FLAB
The Answer Book

Books in This Series

Fitness: The Answer Book by Cecil B. Murphey

Flab: The Answer Book by Jim Krafft, M.D.

Headaches: The Answer Book by Joan Miller, Ph.D.

Heart Attacks: The Answer Book by Daniel J. MacNeil, M.D., and Larry Losoncy, Ph.D.

Junk Food: The Answer Book by Virginia and Norman Rohrer

Vitamins: The Answer Book by Virginia and Norman Rohrer

FLAB
The Answer Book

Jim Krafft, M.D.

SPIRE BOOKS

Fleming H. Revell Company
Old Tappan, New Jersey

Excerpts reprinted by permission from the 1974 "Obesity" special of LIFE AND HEALTH. Copyright © by the Review and Herald Publishing Association.

ISBN: 0-8007-8470-7

Before starting any fitness program, a medical doctor should be consulted.

CONTENTS

1 *The First Word Is Not* Diet   *11*

2 *What Is Fat?*   *16*

3 *How Fat Are You?*   *19*

4 *Why "Fat" Is Sick and "Thin" Is Health*   *24*

5 *How Fat Goes On—and Comes Off*   *29*

6 *How Your Heart Rate Helps You Lose*   *35*

7 *How Often and How Long?*   *39*

8 *When Do I Begin?*   *42*

9 *Who Said It Was Quick and Easy?*   *47*

10 *Why You Should Eat Smart, Not Less*   *52*

11 *You Really Are What You Think!*   *60*

12 *The Power of Setting Goals*   *66*

13 *Why Walking Is a "Perfect" Exercise*   *71*

14 *What Do Other Experts Say?*   *76*

15 *What You Should Know About the "Setpoint Theory"*   *81*

16 *Why Being Well Includes More Than Low Fat Percentage*   *87*

17 *A Final Word on the First Word*   *92*

Source Notes   *94*

For Further Reading   *96*

FLAB
The Answer Book

1

The First Word Is Not *Diet*

How does one get rid of fat? Easy, you say. Just follow Dr. XYZ's super don't-eat-ever diet, and it will all come off rapidly and easily. Success is guaranteed within sixty days or sooner, right?

Wrong! True, you can lose weight on a crash diet. But losing *weight* is not what you who are overfat need to do. You need to get rid of *fat*, not *weight*.

With a crash diet you lose muscle and water and some fat, but confirmed studies show that 99-plus percent of those who lose weight by diet alone will regain it. Not only that, you regain the weight as 100 percent fat! *Crash dieting is one of the surest ways to gain fat, not lose it.* Weight loss by dieting only means you will lose muscle and fat but regain only the fat. Sooner or later you will have a net gain in fat!

It is important to realize that we are all bombarded daily by powerful advertising "hype" about diets and dieting. We have a rash of new miracle diets each year that draw millions of gullible takers. Where I come from we believe in miracles, but the miracle of losing fat comes slowly and steadily in every instance I have ever seen. Sudden hurry-up diets are almost always flagrant examples of bad diet advice.

In "miracle" diets that have been popularized in recent months and years, the dieter's calorie-and-protein intake is cut to starvation levels. True, you can shed pounds quickly with these diets, but while you are battling the bulges of flab, you are running the risk of losing valuable muscle mass that is so important to the entire body, especially the heart. At least one study has shown that such diets have been associated with heart irregularities that resulted in the deaths of fifty-eight women. One popular diet drink provides a daily supply of under 400 calories (starvation level) and less than forty grams of protein (well below the recommended minimum of sixty grams). Persons on this kind of weight-loss plan may experience irregular heart rhythms within a week of starting the diet.

Such miracle diets claim to include vitamin-and-mineral supplements, but they do not alter the bad effects of inadequate dietary protein. Such diets also claim there will be no significant muscle loss, but as a medical doctor who has spent many years in nutritional and weight-control work, I say categorically this is pure hogwash.

The miracle-diet substances or plans preach nutritional nonsense and propagate inaccuracies that can result in life-threatening side effects. For example, one untruth is that undigested food accumulates and becomes fat, while digested food cannot cause weight gain. Precisely the opposite is true. Another myth states that enzymes cannot work together and often cancel each other out in the digestive tract. Again, the facts are exactly the opposite.

In short, *don't use miracle diets!* In the long run they do not work, and they can cause serious harm.

I know what your next question is going to be, and it's a very logical one: "If I can't count on dieting only and miracle diets are downright dangerous, what *can* I do?"

The answer is simple, but it may not thrill you. You don't get rid of fat by diet only. Dieting is important but it is secondary. When trying to lose fat, your primary weapon is aerobic exercise. Aerobic exercise is the kind anyone can do. Aerobic exercises are long, slow, easy, endurance-type activities. I repeat, you do not have to be an Olympic champion to engage in aerobic exercise that fits your abilities and life-style.

So, let's get the cart properly placed *behind* the horse. Exercise (the horse) is first. Diet (the cart) is second.

Please note that when I talk about aerobic exercise, I am not including calisthenics or stretching activities. The exercises you see on TV shows are usually calisthenics or stretching of some kind. These are excellent, but do almost nothing to help you lose fat. Also, spot-reducing aids such as hip-shaker belts at your local health spa do nothing whatsoever to burn fat either, not even in the spot where you are being jostled. When you want to lose fat, engage in aerobic exercise. These are the long, slow, endurance exercises such as walking, jogging, bicycling, and swimming.

As director of Student Health Services at Oral Roberts University for the last ten years, I have seen mild and easy aerobic exercise (note the *mild* and the *easy*) work with hundreds of men and women. Daily, my staff and I guide overfat people in losing weight *and fat*, while toning and building muscles through good nutrition, proper diet,

Just as the horse belongs before the cart, exercise should come before diet.

sports activities, and aerobic exercises that are right for the individual. Yes, it's slower than the miracle crash diets, but it's safer and more effective over the long haul. The weight stays off. There is no regaining of pounds that are composed of more fat than previously.

One example of how our program works is a girl named Helen. She came to school with a severe obesity problem. At five feet six and 178 pounds she could not bring herself to believe that she could ever slow jog one mile. It almost threw her into a tailspin. Our goal is to work individually with each student who is working toward loss of fat, and one day I chose to go on the jogging track with Helen just to help her see that she could do it.

We started going around the track at more of a walk than a jog. Helen kept saying, "I can't do it," and I kept encouraging her by saying, "Slow to a walk and just keep going, just keep going, just keep going."

With continual encouragement, Helen covered the full mile that day, doing far more walking than jogging. She was so motivated by her achievement that she began to engage enthusiastically in our fat-loss program. After four and a half months she had lost forty pounds. She got so enthusiastic about jogging that she started overdoing it and had to stop running for a brief time because of sore muscles. She did not, however, significantly regain any of the forty pounds that she had lost. When she was able to resume her exercise program, she combined it with proper eating and soon was down to her ideal fat level. (By "ideal fat level" I mean a correct percentage of body fat. We'll look more at this in chapter three.)

Helen, by the way, is a good example of the important fringe benefits in a fat-loss program. When she started, she was withdrawn, antisocial, and depressed. As she engaged in the program and achieved success, she became an exhilarated, joyful person.

Right about now you may be thinking, *Hurray for Helen. I've heard about these jogging freaks before. I just can't see jogging several miles a day. I don't have the time, and I really don't have the ambition. Furthermore, Helen was a college kid and I'm an adult. This aerobic stuff is okay for kids, but not for older types like me.*

Okay, I hear you, but remember, Helen started slowly—*very* slowly. For many days she walked more than she jogged. Actually she could have achieved the same results by *walking only.* It would have taken a little longer, but the results would have been the same.

As for aerobics being "only for kids," nothing is further from the truth. People of *any age* can participate in the long, slow, endurance type of aerobic exercise at their own speed and in their own way.

So, in *Flab: The Answer Book*, the first word to emphasize is *exercise*—slow, easy, aerobic exercise. Healthy, sensible exercise must become a permanent part of your life-style. Control of weight and fat is a lifetime proposition. The joys of an active life-style with sensible diet make it more than worthwhile.

Still skeptical? I won't try to kid you or lie to you. Controlling weight and fat *permanently* takes effort, but anyone can do it at his or her own speed. To do so you need to understand some simple principles about what fat is and why it is so dangerous. In layman's terms, I can tell you how to have the right percentage of fat on your body and how aerobic exercise works to burn off unneeded fat and keep it off.

Read on—you may have a lot to lose!

2

What Is Fat?

Fat is the oily, greasy substance that we all want to get rid of. People who are fat talk about their "weight problem" or "being a little heavy." Ironically, the heavy stuff on our frame is the good stuff—the muscle. Fat is light, not heavy, and that is one of the reasons I say the problem is not being *overweight;* with most of us it's being *overfat.*

Fat accumulates on your body predominantly in two places: just under the skin (subcutaneous fat) and in the muscles. You can't see the fat in your muscles, but it looks exactly like the fat in an ideal steak that is "marbled" with just enough streaks of fat to make it taste wonderful. (Too much marbled steak, by the way, is a tasty but surefire way to consume too much fat in your diet.)

Subcutaneous fat, on the other hand, settles just under the skin on your stomach, waist, hips, legs, and arms. It is easy to see but hard to get rid of.

That extra flab that we would like to see melt away from our stomach, waist, and hips is caused by our fat cells (adipocytes). We all have a certain number of fat cells that are established by the time we reach adolescence. Once that number of fat cells is reached, it stabilizes and we don't add anymore. Overeating does not increase the number of your fat cells; it merely increases the fat in the cells that you already have.

So, the bad news is that once we establish our number of fat cells, we have them for life. Fat people have 190 percent more fat cells than slender types. Flab fighters also have fat cells that are forty percent larger than the fat cells in slender people.

Now, I can hear some people saying, "Oh, that's it— that's my problem. I have too many fat cells, and there's nothing I can do. I'll just have to be heavy and live with it. Please pass the pie."

Not so! The good news is that although you can't reduce *the number* of fat cells in your body, you can reduce *the size* of your fat cells. Your goal is to have "skinny" fat cells, and you reach that goal with aerobic exercise and a sensible diet. As the diagram on page 13 shows, you need the cart and the horse in the right order. And you need them both to take off flab and keep it off.

Understandably, one way we all put on too much flab is by eating too much fat. Unfortunately, fat is found in many of the tasty snacks we love to munch. That's why it becomes such a problem in regard to our total intake of calories.

Keep in mind that one gram of fat has nine calories, while a gram of carbohydrate or protein has only four calories. This means that if you eat a pound of butter, which is practically 100 percent fat, you consume about 3,500 calories. It takes 3,500 calories to add one pound of body weight. Therefore, simple arithmetic says that if you eat a pound of butter and don't burn any of it off, you will put on a pound of fat. To lose one pound of fat you must either burn 3,500 calories or eat 3,500 fewer calories than your normal daily requirement.

Because fat has more than twice the calories contained in carbohydrate or protein, it is the most effective fuel your body can burn. The trick is to consume enough fat for your body to use as fuel, but not to eat too much and start storing it in your subcutaneous tissue or in your muscles. We can learn that secret, but our bodies need to be taught *how* to burn fat with the correct amount of aerobic exercise. We'll explore that subject in chapter fifteen, which discusses your body's "setpoint," and how you can "retrain your enzymes."

There's one other way to answer the question "What is fat?" It may sound dramatic but it is true: *Fat is a killer.* Being too fat can cause angina, high blood pressure, congestive heart failure, intermittent claudication (a form of pain in the lower extremities), varicose veins, intervertebral disc disease, osteoarthritis, gall bladder disease, diabetes, asthma, and hyperlipidemia (which is increased fat substances in the blood). All of these diseases and disorders can influence everything from disability to premature death.

In respect to the human body, then, fat is many things, and most of them are bad. It is true that we need some fat. In correct amounts fat is a useful food. In fact, if you get too little fat in your diet, this can also lead to problems. For example, women who have too low a fat intake fail to menstruate.

But for the vast majority of us the problem is too much fat in our bodies, not too little. In the next chapter we will take a look at how much fat is enough and how to measure your own fat content.

3

How Fat Are You?

How fat are you? Because you live in today's mechanized society, chances are your percentage of body fat is higher than it ought to be. In precivilized times, it was necessary that the human organism store large amounts of fat in order for it to survive long seasons when food was not readily available. In the conditions of life today in industrialized countries, however, the accumulation of fat no longer serves any useful purpose. It is just something extra to carry around.

"So, how do I know I'm carrying a lot of extra flab?" you may ask. "How can I know just how 'overfat' I am?"

Dr. Covert Bailey, author of the excellent book *Fit or Fat?*, has done extensive studies with people of all ages and body structures.[1] He concludes that the ideal amount of body fat for an adult male is 15 percent; and for a female, 22 percent. According to other extensive research, the ideal body fat for an athlete in professional, or serious amateur, competition is 11 percent for males and 17 percent for women.

I'm not quite sure why nonathletes should be allowed a higher percentage of body fat than athletes. Perhaps ideal goals would be the 11 to 17 percent range for males and the 17 to 22 percent range for females.

Unfortunately, most people have body-fat percentages well above the recommended norms. Dr. Bailey's findings show that the average male has 24 percent body fat and the average female has 33 percent. Dr. Bailey believes that these figures are much too high, and anyone with 24 or 33 percent body fat or above is in the category of "sick," or at least facing high susceptibility to illness. For example, his findings show that males with body fat above 24 percent suffer from fat deposits in their arteries. Fat deposits in your arteries are what help cause high blood pressure, arterial sclerosis, and, in extreme cases, a myocardial infarction (heart attack).

If you are interested in trivia, the highest percentage of body fat ever measured on a human is 68 percent. You're probably well below that extreme, but you are also probably somewhere over the ideal norm of 11 to 17 percent for men and 17 to 22 percent for women.

How can you measure your percentage of body fat? There are two basic methods: underwater weighing, which is the most accurate; and skin-fold measurements.

Underwater weighing is best because you get a *total* estimate of the fat in your body. As I mentioned in chapter two, fat accumulates in our muscles and in the subcutaneous tissue just under the skin. Because fat is light, it tends to float and can be measured quite accurately by underwater weighing, which takes special equipment. Ironically, the lighter you are under water, the more fat your body contains. Underwater weighing equipment is becoming available at some YMCAs, as well as in some fitness centers, physicians' clinics, and in some high schools and colleges.

A more available method of estimating body-fat percentage is skin-fold measurement, usually done with calipers that "pinch" (hold together lightly) the skin in spots where fat tends to form in the subcutaneous tissues. You may have heard of the simple "rule of thumb" test anyone can do. With your thumb and forefinger pinch the skin on your waist, just above your pelvic (hip) bone. If the fold of skin—and fat—exceeds one inch, you are carrying too much body fat.

In our fitness and health center at Oral Roberts University we measure with calipers, which are applied to the front of the upper arm (bicep area), behind the upper arm (tricep area), behind the shoulder blade, and at the waist just above the pelvic bone. After measuring with the calipers, we calculate body-fat percentage with a formula provided by the caliper manufacturer. If you are interested in trying this yourself, you can buy calipers and complete instructions for under twenty-five dollars. Or, it might be simpler to find a medical doctor, YMCA, or fitness center that uses caliper measurements. Another means of measurement available at some Ys and fitness centers is done with a caliper that includes an electronic device called "Skyndex," which requires no special calculations.

To summarize, the ideal way to measure body-fat percentage is with underwater weighing, which measures fat in the muscles and under the skin. Less accurate, but still fairly reliable, is skin-fold measurement of the fat under the skin, done with calipers or an automatically computing caliper like "Skyndex."

If you are at all serious about fighting flab and getting your percentage of body fat down to correct levels, get measured where and how you can. Whatever you do, don't depend on the old familiar height/weight tables to determine fatness. Until recent years these height/weight tables were the best information available and have been promoted by health and life insurance companies with the best of intentions. But today much better methods are available.

It is quite possible for some individuals to be heavily muscled and "overweight" according to the height/weight tables. Every so often we get someone in our center who has excellent muscle tone and muscle mass, but who is anywhere from ten to thirty pounds over what he is supposed to weigh at his height according to the tables.

A recent example is a young fellow I'll call Sam, who was among the new crop of students at ORU. At nineteen years of age, Sam was a good twenty pounds "overweight" according to the height/weight tables. Yet, Sam's body was so firm and hard that we could not measure it with calipers.

"What was your sport in high school, Sam?" I asked.

Sam replied that he hadn't played any high-school sports, but he had been on the power-lifting team at the athletic center in his town. He added that he also did some jogging.

We measured Sam underwater and found that he had a body fat content of only 6 percent!

Granted, people like Sam are rare exceptions. The typical person has a higher fat percentage than what is desirable. To repeat Dr. Covert Bailey's research findings, desirable fat percentage in the male is around 15 percent and in the female, 22 percent. (My own personal estimates include a little broader range: 11 to 17 percent for males and 17 to 22 percent for females.) Bailey's studies also showed that the average male has a 24 percent fat content and the average female, 33 percent—much higher than desirable.

So, if your doctor or a technician at the Y or at a fitness center weighs or measures you, and you find that your fat content is too high, don't despair or think that you are one of the unusual few who are in this condition. All of the research and experience of those who are in the field of fitness and weight and fat control show that up to 50 million Americans are significantly overfat.

And don't forget that the height/weight guidelines do not give an accurate picture. Most of us would be far better off if we spent no time studying height/weight tables and became concerned only with our fat-percentage content. A person can be just the right weight for his height (according to the height/weight tables) and still be plagued with flab and a fat percentage that is too high.

An example of this is a girl I will call Gloria. At eighteen, Gloria was a college student who was driven by the need to maintain a "Twiggy-like figure." She dieted constantly and was always worried about "getting too fat." At five feet four inches and 105 pounds, Gloria looked quite slender, but when we examined her, we discovered that her body was surprisingly flabby. Caliper measurements revealed that she had a body fat content of 27 percent!

We urged Gloria to go into an aerobic program and to start eating sensibly. She did so and was soon making progress toward a much firmer body. She also got over her anxieties about gaining too much weight.

Gloria is a striking example of someone who seemed to be the right weight for her height. She even looked quite slender at first glance. But her body fat content was much too high. Other overfat people who come into our health center are easier to spot. They weigh in at what seems to be an acceptable figure for their height, but it is easy to see that they have quite a bit of flab in the usual spots—stomach, waist, arms, and legs. These same people often complain of a lack of energy and stamina. And it almost always follows that they have not been maintaining any kind of proper program of muscle activity.

Maintaining proper muscle activity (getting proper exercise) is the name of the game. If you don't play that game, you are most certainly in danger of getting fatter and fatter. True, you may be one of the blessed ones, who don't have as many fat cells (see chapter two) or you may have the kind of metabolism that allows you to eat all you want and "never gain an ounce." But, if you are such a person, chances are you wouldn't even bother to read this book. You are reading this book because you are concerned about flab and how to get rid of it. Contrary to myths and clichés that we've all heard, fat is bad, never "healthy," "strong," or the source of a "jolly good fellow." In the next chapter I'll explain why fat is so dangerous and why "thin is health."

4

Why "Fat" Is Sick and "Thin" Is Health

One of the biggest challenges (and frustrations) I face in my work is convincing people how serious overfatness can be. Many people I talk to regard fat as a simple cosmetic problem. They come in wanting to drop a couple of dress sizes or lose a few inches from the waist. What I keep trying to tell them is—*fatness is a killer.* Obesity—even being "mildly overfat"—is a disease that requires attention and treatment.

I often hear the argument: "Why get so worked up over a few extra pounds and a few extra folds of skin? Everyone knows that as you get older the weight gets redistributed. So, I'm a little heavier than I'd like to be and my 'love handlebars' are easy to spot. A little dieting, a little working out and I'll be fine."

Not necessarily. Fatness seems to have what scientists call a "threshold." Even a few pounds above this threshold can cause all kinds of health hazards. There is a danger zone for weight and fatness, and many people are into that danger zone without realizing it. A goodly number of these same people develop serious problems, some of which could even be fatal. Following is a brief list of the hazards you are risking by carrying "those few (or quite a few) extra pounds":

- Fat people have higher levels of blood lipids, which are fats and oils in the blood that increase the risk of heart disease or stroke.
- Fat people have a much stronger tendency to have that "silent" problem—high blood pressure.
- Fat people suffer more often from coronary heart disease.
- Extra weight may bring on diabetes in persons susceptible to this disease.
- Fat women suffer more often from gynecological irregularities; obese pregnant women are more likely to have toxemia, which leads to serious complications.
- Fat people have more complications and problems during and after surgery.
- Also, carrying around a load of extra fat (even a few pounds) strains the bones and joints and can accentuate arthritis, especially in the knees, hips, and lower spine.
- Excess fat strains the muscles of the abdominal wall (belly), sometimes giving rise to formation of abdominal hernias.
- Increased and adverse amounts of fat in and around the muscles of the legs slows blood return through the veins to the heart, which is a factor in precipitating varicose veins.
- A fatty chest can cause difficulty in breathing.
- Gout is much more common in obese persons.
- There is even a marked increase in accidents among the severely obese.

The old concept of the happy fat person has been

thoroughly disproved. In fact, fat people are much more susceptible to depression.

If all of the above problems were not enough, there are also well-known social, and even economic, disadvantages to being fat. A fat person: (1) is less likely to be sought after as a marriage partner; (2) pays higher insurance premiums; (3) meets discrimination when applying for a job; (4) cannot find attractive clothing as easily; (5) is limited in choice of sports and activities.

Nationwide, fat girls have only one-third the chance of being accepted into college that lean girls have. (I'm happy to say that at Oral Roberts University this is not the case.) Even during early childhood years, a fat youngster often suffers severe ridicule from classmates and the humiliation of being chosen last for games.

I could go on, but you get the point. Being fat is a *severe* handicap—physically, mentally, and emotionally. Our society, consciously or unconsciously, is becoming more and more punitive toward the fat person. For example, according to the studies of Dr. Jean Mayer, obese adolescent girls suffer from heightened sensitivity, obsessive concerns, passivity, and withdrawal. All of these traits are similar to those of minorities who are subjected to intense prejudice.

Studies done on our ORU campus also confirm the disadvantages of overfatness. As part of her work on a master's degree, Barbara C. O'Conner, a nurse practitioner, did research on the effects of body fat on the health of a group of ORU coeds. She conducted her study for one entire school year, approximately nine months, and carefully logged each student's health record and number of visits to the health clinic. Visits to the clinic were counted and classified in two categories: medical and athletically related.

At the beginning of the study all of the 357 freshmen women involved were measured for body-fat percentages by the skin-fold estimate method. Fifty-seven percent of the women had a body fat content above 26 percent.

Forty-three percent had a body fat content below 26 percent. If you remember Dr. Covert Bailey's figures (see chapter three), the ideal body fat content for a typical woman is 22 percent, with very active female athletes having as little as 17 percent. For purposes of her study, Barbara O'Conner decided to give women in the 22 to 26 percent body-fat range the benefit of the doubt. Anyone above 26 percent of body fat, however, she termed "overfat" to a greater or lesser degree. This means that in the study of 357 coeds, 57 percent were in the overfat range with body fat of 26 percent or higher. In that overfat group approximately 70 of the women were measured at figures that Barbara chose to term as obese—anywhere from 30 to 42 percent body fat.

During the nine-month study, 76 percent of the students in the overfat group visited the Student Health Service Clinic. During that same period, only 58 percent of the women in the group with body fat under 26 percent visited the clinic. Barbara O'Conner also recorded that visits to the clinic for athletics-related injuries were significantly higher in the overfat group. Thirty-six percent of the overfat coeds made clinic visits for athletics-related injuries while only 19 percent of the students with less than 26 percent body fat made such clinic visits.

In summary, Barbara O'Conner's study showed a measurable correlation between percentage of body fat and health. Those students with a higher percentage of body fat were adversely affected. The overfat were significantly more ill than the underfat. In addition, the injuries and illnesses of the overfat population were more serious and more debilitating than those of the group who could be considered "normally fat."

Most significantly, women students with body fat of 30 percent and above were the least-healthy group.[1]

So far most of the news in this chapter has been bad. I wrote it this way to dramatize and underline one basic fact: Being overfat, or as many of us like to put it, "carrying a few extra pounds," is definitely unhealthy. The good news, however, is that obesity is always reversible. You don't have to stay fat. You can rid yourself of your fat before serious problems set in. Once you get rid of your fat, you can look forward to just as long and healthy a life as the skinny types who never had to battle flab. Studies show that mortality rates are not any higher for people who were formerly fat than for those who were never fat.

Assuming you are convinced you have at least some fat to lose, the next question is obvious. What do you do about it? Most of the remainder of this book deals with what might be called one basic physical law. Violate this law and flab will almost always form in ample amounts on your body.

You may have heard of Murphy's law: "If anything can go wrong it probably will." Krafft's physical law of aerobics states: "Fat accumulates in direct proportion to the amount of time spent moving jaws rather than legs and feet."

Some people like exercise; some can take it or leave it; and some hate it. But we *all* need it. Stick with me and I'll show you how to work out an exercise life-style you can live with—much longer.

5

How Fat Goes On—and Comes Off

"I can't understand it. I eat like a bird and still can't lose an ounce."

You may have heard a complaint like that from a friend. Maybe you've muttered the same lament yourself. At the ORU Student Health Service I hear this kind of remark quite often. I smile understandingly and try to explain that all of us find it easy to fool ourselves. The hard truth is, fat accumulates when caloric intake exceeds calorie output. To put it another way, we get fat by eating more and exercising less.

In the pioneer days of our nation obesity was not a major problem. It's true that back then people didn't know as much about nutrition. They ate far too much fat. But for the most part men and women had to put in many hours of physical labor, which burned off the extra calories that they consumed. The big factor in keeping people fit and

We get fat by eating more and exercising less.

relatively thin was the healthful amount of physical activity they had to engage in each day.

As we have become more "civilized," we have lost many good things that a more natural life-style provided. A back-to-the-country, back-to-the-farm, back-to-nature type of life-style would automatically help us to exercise more intensively, and just as automatically we would solve a lot of obesity problems. But we enjoy our technological goodies too much. We jump into the automobile to go three blocks to the corner grocery store. We turn on the television set rather than enjoying a walk in the beauty of

God's outdoors. And while we watch television, advertising bombards us every few minutes urging us to head for the refrigerator to get snacks and drinks in order to "enjoy the program more."

Calories do count, and they count up fast. Depending on your job and life-style, you need a certain minimum number of calories per day. In fact, we all burn a basic number of basal calories every day and night, no matter how much or little work we do. For men the basal number of calories is 1,600, for women it's 1,500.[1] Then, depending on how active we are, we burn additional calories per day as we walk about, dial the phone, yawn, take out the trash, yes, and even while we drive the car. (Naturally, a stick shift takes a few more calories than an automatic.)

According to the Food and Nutrition Board, National Research Council, the recommended calorie allowances per day for a 154-pound man are as follows:

Sedentary—2,500 calories
Moderately active—3,000 calories
Very active—3,500 calories
For a 123-pound woman the calorie allowance is:
Sedentary—2,100 calories
Moderately active—2,500 calories
Very active—3,000 calories[2]

(Note: For each decade over the age of twenty, these numbers should be reduced.)

For all of us weight and fat control is a simple matter of "energy in and energy out." All you have to do to gain a pound a week is simply fail to burn off 500 excess calories each day. By "excess" I mean calories over and above the amount you need acccording to your job and activity schedule. For example, that 154-pound man with a sedentary occupation needs 2,500 calories per day. If he continually puts away 3,000 per day and doesn't burn off that extra 500, it wouldn't be hard at all to gain 50 pounds in a year.

Most of us have a fairly good understanding of what I've covered above. We know that we should only take in so many calories per day and that when we "pig out," we gain weight. Just talk to anyone when they come back to work after vacation. They will usually tell you they gained five to ten pounds, because they ate so much more than usual while they "took it easy" (i.e., sat around).

Many of us go through the calendar year playing the dieting game. We overeat during vacation and then try to lose the weight gained. We overeat during Christmas season and then try to lose that. And so it goes. We struggle and struggle not to eat. We keep looking for the latest-and-best new diet or scheme or "miracle plan" to keep our weight under control.

And it's true, you can lose weight and fat by dieting; many people do. But as I said earlier, the chances are good to excellent you will put that weight back on in the form of more fat than before. And, as I also said before—and will say again and again—the *only* way to take off fat and *keep it off* is through aerobic exercise.

The immediate question is, "Well then, what is aerobic exercise?" The word *aerobic* means "with oxygen," or "with air." During aerobic exercise the body burns up its fuel (calories) by utilizing oxygen taken in through the lungs. Aerobic exercise is long, slow, endurance type exercise. It means continuously exercising without pauses. This is crucial. That is why I have listed swimming, bicycling, running, jogging, and walking as excellent aerobic exercises.

The opposite of aerobic exercise is what is called anaerobic exercise, which is defined as "exercise not requiring oxygen." Short sprints and dashes, or brief, but mighty, efforts to lift weights are examples of anaerobic exercise. Yes, these activities take some oxygen, but the oxygen is not consumed by the aerobic-burning process inside the body's cells. To get your body into "aerobic gear," so to speak, you need the long, steady pumping of air through the lungs, which happens when you go for a brisk two-mile walk or a five-mile jog.

Anaerobic—short-term, overexertional—exercises do

not contribute to weight loss and are much more likely to cause injury. Look in any book on aerobics and you will see that sports like tennis, handball, baseball, football, and even basketball are described as only fair aerobic activity. That's because all of these sports take short bursts of exertion, but then also include periods of stopping, standing, and in the case of baseball, even sitting between innings.

Any amount of exercise has some benefit, of course, but the really important exercise as far as losing fat is concerned is the continuous movement, where you *keep going*. It is right here where we labor with a common misconception. From earliest childhood many of us are admonished to run hard, go fast, get after it, get it over with quickly. This kind of mind-set actually works against us when we are attempting aerobic—long, slow, continuous—exercise to lose fat.

Hal Higdon, a friend of mine, is an outstanding author as well as a very active aerobic runner. In a recent article for a national publication Hal said this: "If you want to lose weight, the slower you run the better."[3] Hal's remark is a colorful way to underline what I've been trying to say. The body metabolizes (burns off) fat more efficiently during exercise done at slow speeds. *Gentle exercise,* whether running, swimming, cycling, or just walking, burns fat more efficiently than brief fast-paced exercise.

The key is to keep at it—for at least thirty minutes or more. Obviously, slow, gentle walking or jogging for thirty seconds isn't going to do you much good. Tests suggest that a jogger who is moving at a slow, submaximal pace obtains as much as 50 to 60 percent of his energy from body fat. So, the trick is to take it easy, or as one outstanding older runner has said, "Start slowly, then taper off."

I realize that if you are one of those people who hate exercise, the thought of any aerobic activity is not going to send thrills of anticipation up and down your spine. But without aerobic activity your battle against flab will continue to be a losing one and by "losing" I mean you will keep *gaining* fat instead of getting rid of it and keeping it off. That's why I keep emphasizing the idea that aerobic exercise can be gentle, easy, and slow. Exercise physiologists tell us that excellent benefits can be achieved by going slower—and without most of the strains that sometimes come with jogging and running.

In other words, you do not have to become a marathon runner to engage in pleasant, easy aerobic exercise. All you need to do is get your heart rate up a little higher than it beats while you are sitting in the car or leaning back in front of the TV set. This is good for your heart and also burns off fat. We'll look at how all this works in the next chapter.

6

How Your Heart Rate
Helps You Lose

In the preceding chapter we talked about how and why aerobic exercise gets rid of fat. I stressed that aerobic exercise should be slow and easy, but it must be carried on long enough and hard enough to do the job. Your exercise intensity, or how hard you are working, is best determined by your pulse or heart rate. You need a target or training heart rate at which you should do your fat-losing exercises. Simply stated, it is best to exercise at an intensity of 70 to 85 percent of your maximum heart rate.

What is your maximum heart rate? You estimate your heart rate by subtracting your age from 220. At almost 60 years of age, I estimate my maximum heart rate at 220 minus 60 or 160 beats per minute—the rate at which my heart would beat if I were working at full capacity.

To determine my exercise or training heart rate I simply multiply my maximum heart rate by seven-tenths or 70 percent. Therefore, my training heart rate is 70 percent of 160 or 112 beats per minute. The estimate of 112 isn't a figure that has to be precise. It only has to be within a target range. The target range I'm after for a training heart rate is between 70 and 85 percent of my maximum, so I should exercise at somewhere between 112 to 136 beats per minute. A top figure of 136 beats is, of course, 85 percent of my theoretical maximum heart rate of 160.

What is the best way to count your heart rate? Taking a pulse is simple and easy for some persons, but a little more difficult for others. The best way is to reach with your left hand, palm side down, over to the thumb side of your right wrist and press down with three fingers. Just above the wrist you can feel the artery pumping in the groove between the bone of the thumb side and the tendon nearby. The sweep second hand on your wristwatch should be in plain view on your left wrist.

Once you have found your pulse, count it for only six seconds of that sweep second hand on your wristwatch. Six seconds will be ideal because you can simply add a zero to it to estimate your pulse rate.

To get a good idea of your training pulse rate (70 to 85 percent of maximum) walk or jog a block or two, then stop and immediately take your pulse. Suppose you are forty years old. That means you're looking for the pace that will produce 126 beats per minute. (Remember the formula: 220 minus 40 equals 180 times seven-tenths equals 126.)

Some persons can count while they are walking or running, but I can't; I have to stop. It is important, though, to count your pulse right away. Don't wait a minute or two until your heart slows down somewhat because then you would not have an accurate figure. Get the number of pulse beats per six seconds and add a zero. That figure is a good estimate of your training pulse rate.

Remember you are aiming for a range from 70 to 85 percent of your maximum heart rate, and it does not have to be an exact number. As you become used to checking your pulse you will find that you can estimate it readily in six seconds as you pause during or right after your walk, run, or whatever exercise you are doing.

Heart rate is the best indication of whether or not you are doing your exercise at the proper intensity. If you are significantly overfat, you will find that your pulse, even during a moderate walk, quickly reaches the training heart range of 70 to 85 percent of maximum. As you become trained and shed fat, the amount of effort necessary to get the pulse into the training range will gradually increase. Much later on you may even find you have to break into a jog to reach a heart rate in the training zone.

I dealt recently with a thirty-seven-year-old pastor who had returned to school to get a master's degree. He was typically out of shape, but nonetheless he tried to start his program by jogging immediately. But any amount of jogging sent his pulse rate to over 200, which was above his recommended maximum of 183 beats per minute (220 minus 37).

I told him firmly, "*Walk only* for the first few weeks. Jogging is out for you until you get in better shape." He did as I instructed and walked only for almost three weeks. Later on he started mixing a little jogging with the walking. Eventually he was jogging at a slow pace and enjoying his proper training rate, which was around 128 to 155 beats per minute.

So, now you see how aerobic exercise is easily measured by heart rate. Take 220 minus your age and then 70 to 85 percent of that number. If you exercise in this range and do not try to exceed it, you benefit in two crucial ways:

1. You will be exercising safely.
2. You will be exercising at the most effective level for getting rid of fat.

But some obvious questions remain. If you are like most of the people I deal with at the ORU Health Service, you are concerned about the time all this takes. How often should you exercise? How long or far should you walk, run, swim, or bike? Turn the page and get the good news. In less than fifteen minutes you can start burning off the fat forever!

7

How Often and How Long?

Aerobic exercise must be continued long enough for the oxygen we breathe to burn excess food stores, particularly the fat on our bodies. In his book *Fit or Fat?* Covert Bailey estimates that twelve minutes is a minimum for continuous exercise to be effective. This is certainly not an ideal amount of time, but whenever you can exercise continuously for at least twelve minutes you will be into the range at which some fat loss can occur.

As to the "ideal" amount of time, most authorities say about thirty minutes five times a week should maintain and slowly improve fitness along with significantly resulting in the loss of fat—if you need to lose. Research shows that if you exercise fewer than three days a week, however, the fitness effect will regress.

From my work at the ORU Health Service, I believe the ideal schedule is one hour at least three times a week of endurance exercise and a shorter period—about thirty minutes—on three other days. My personal aerobic program includes a schedule of six days a week, and I usually alternate with one-hour and half-hour workouts.

I use a phrase with my students that is certainly true for me, and it may be true for you: "I am so extremely busy that I cannot afford to jog or walk *less* than one hour at least three times a week." I firmly believe this because of the mental-health benefits that are also important in aerobic exercise. I really need that full hour three or more days a week to regroup my attitudes and release my tensions.

Remember that with aerobic exercise the emphasis is on time, not distance or speed. If you want to shape up fast, exercise longer, not harder. To review, an aerobic exercise:

1. Lasts a minimum of twelve minutes
2. Maintains your heart rate at 70 to 85 percent of maximum for the entire time
3. Should be done a minimum of three days a week—and six is ideal
4. Is steady and nonstop

Covert Bailey states that if he were obese (as he once was), he would walk three to four hours per day to get the fat off.

If six days of exercise is good, is seven better? To be motivated enough to exercise seven days a week is commendable. However, our Lord rested one day during creation, and it is a good rule for us to do the same. Perhaps God set that example because He knew something that we didn't about "burn out."

To sum up, the absolute ideal for exercise is six days a week, scheduled at a specific time each day. That way it becomes a part of your life—something you genuinely look forward to each day six days a week.

The next question might be whether you need to continue exercising for six months or a full year. It's easy to answer that one. The program should become part of your life-style and should continue as long as you are in good health and strength. There is no age limit on aerobic exercise. The oldest person I worked with is a lady of sixty-seven. She ran her first marathon at the age of sixty-five. I know of several people in their seventies who run marathons. Let me remind you that a marathon is a little over twenty-six miles!

A healthful life-style means continuing effective aerobic exercise as long as one lives. And the whole idea behind aerobic exercise is to help you live longer and healthier. As I like to tell my students at the ORU Health Service, "Personally I want to die young, but as late in life as possible."

If you have stuck with me to this point, you may be ready to give aerobic exercise a try. (On the other hand, you may have already started or perhaps you have tried it, stopped for a while, and aren't sure if you want to try it again.) When should you begin? Well, how about right now?

8

When Do I Begin?

If not right now, how about right after work tomorrow? Get out some comfortable clothes, tie on those super-cushioned jogging shoes (or any good walking shoes) and go out the door!

Even this first time, be sure to keep going for at least twelve minutes, but don't push it. Your motto is "easy does it." Watch your pulse and don't get it over the limit of 70 to 85 percent of your maximum heart rate. Be extra careful and do not move too much or too fast this first time.

You may be wondering about the need for a doctor's physical exam. This is usually not necessary if you make a gentle beginning by simply walking. You should be having regular checkups by a physician already, with a complete exam at least every three years. Few doctors will forbid something as easy as walking; in fact, most doctors will encourage it. If your doctor says no and you believe you are healthy, you might get a second opinion from another physician. It always helps to find a doctor who walks or jogs himself. Unless you have a really serious problem, you

Brisk walking can reduce flab and build muscle tone along with self-esteem.

should get the green light for participating in aerobic exercise on a sensible basis.

I often suggest to people that they begin their aerobic program in the evening after work to release tensions that have cropped up during the day. But any time is the right time of day to begin your exercise program. The important factor is that it's the right time for *you.* For homemakers, how about early-morning hours? It's inspiring to me to go out into the cool of early morning and see pairs of women briskly walking away the flab and building good muscle tone along with high self-esteem.

These women are living proof that walking is the number-one sport for just about anyone. All sorts of fancy and expensive "toys" are marketed as the latest answers to exercise and losing weight. Almost all of them are useless as far as fat-losing aerobics is concerned. Why bother with these gadgets? God gave us two marvelous appendages called feet. Walking is a delightful way to use those feet, especially if you can walk outdoors. As long as you make sure your heart doesn't race out of control, it is nearly impossible to overtrain or harm yourself by walking. Few of us do not have access to a surface upon which we can walk, and walking requires no specialized equipment.

If you can afford them, it is a good idea to buy a pair of well-cushioned jogging shoes that fit and support your feet correctly. Please don't use tennis shoes, "deck" shoes, or other "sneaker" types of footwear. The modern, well-developed jogging shoe is a great invention, and you will be amazed at the difference it makes, whether you are running or walking.

You may be wondering what I do for aerobic exercise. Running or walking? I admit to being a slow jogger, but the chief reason is that I have become too fit to get my heart rate up to the proper speed by walking. I must jog or run in order to reach 70 to 85 percent of maximum heart rate.

I particularly enjoy the fun of competing in distance races in a "noncompetitive" manner. I say noncompetitive because racing is just as much fun if I finish last.

A word of caution is in order about exercising in extreme heat. If you are beginning your program in hot weather (90 degrees or above), take your time and go only very short distances at first. Even though I am in excellent condition, when the thermometer registers over 100, I return to walking and still get to enjoy the outdoors even when the temperature is sizzling.

What happens if you enjoy and prefer walking but get into such good shape that you have a hard time getting your heart to training range? One answer is to use a backpack with gradually increasing loads. Another possibility is speed or race walking, which is appealing to a growing number of devotees. Always take care to watch your heart rate to ensure that you are not overdoing it but that you are getting into the training range.

If walking seems a bit tame for you, try other outstanding aerobic sports like bicycling, swimming, cross-country skiing, or aerobic dance. Granted, you can run into problems as you search for variety or something more exciting than walking. Snow is not always available for skiing. Many of us don't have access to a swimming pool on a daily basis. It is sometimes hard to find a path or road where you can bicycle for any distance in safety.

Rhythmic aerobics or aerobic dance is great, but there is usually too much bounce in this sport for the overfat person, at least in the beginning. Your best bet is to walk for a while and then try rhythmic aerobics and other challenging activities.

By the way, swimming is one of the best of sports for conditioning, and it is especially beneficial to people with orthopedic problems in their muscles, joints, or bones. Ironically, however, it is not the best activity for losing extra fat under the skin. Swimming takes fat out of your muscles, to be sure, but do not expect to readily note your fat loss by pinching skin if you are a swimmer. The body keeps a certain amount of subskin fat to protect it from cool water.

Joseph Moreno is a good example of what swimming can do. He came to us at 236 pounds, with a severe knee problem and 29.6 percent body fat, according to underwater weighing. He went into a swimming program that included one-half to one mile per day at a slow, steady, aerobic pace. By mid-term, underwater weighing registered his body fat at 23.8 percent, but his weight had only dropped one pound. By the end of the year, however, his weight had dropped to 215, and underwater weighing showed his body fat at 22 percent, a drop of 7.6 percent over nine months, which we consider excellent results.

At no time during the year did we try to estimate Joseph's body fat with skin calipers. He kept a typical swimmer's sleek appearance with the extra layer of fat under the skin. Where he lost the most body fat, however, was in his muscles. He left our obesity-level class and continued swimming on his own with a goal of getting his body fat below 20 percent.

Let me say once more that sports like golf, tennis, bowling, racquetball, and the like are all good, but they just do not qualify for the job of burning fat through aerobics. All of these sports have too much intermittency, that is, standing around between plays or action. These sports do not provide *continuous* activity. It's a good idea to walk or jog to get in shape *to* play these sports. But do not try to get in shape *by* playing golf, tennis, softball, and so forth.

Other ways to engage in aerobic activity include cycling on a stationary bike or running in place on a mini-trampoline. Many persons, including my beloved wife, LaVerne, find such aerobic activities just the thing. One attractive feature of stationary cycling or running in place on a trampoline is that they can be done in air-conditioned or heated comfort. To bike or jog in place would be boring for me—but to each his own. Any exercise that you enjoy which is continuous and uses large muscle groups will do the job. For most of us, especially those who are definitely obese, walking will usually be the ideal way to begin.

Therefore, if you are reasonably well physically, today is the best day to begin your program. If something comes up to frustrate you, don't berate yourself. To paraphrase the lead song from a hit musical, "Tomorrow's aerobics are just a day away!"

9

Who Said It Was Quick and Easy?

Not me, that's for sure. People who say that losing fat is quick and easy are telling an unmitigated untruth. It takes time and it takes continuous effort to lose fat and keep it lost.

Advertisements on TV, radio, and in newspapers and magazines tell us we can lose quickly and easily through special diets and devices like belts and massage machines and gadgets. All of this is just not true or is vastly over-rated.

Yes, you can lose four or five pounds "overnight" by sweating out water or taking a diuretic that prompts your kidneys to get rid of the water in a hurry. But this has nothing to do with losing actual fat. As soon as you drink normal amounts of water again—which you should do just to stay healthy—that "lost" four or five pounds will be mysteriously found again. As for crash dieting, I have already pointed out that while you can lose weight, the odds are overwhelmingly in favor of your regaining it with a net gain in fat once you do put the lost pounds back on (see chapter one).

My own fat-loss program has extended over ten years. Admittedly, I was not completely out of control at the start, but at 206 pounds and body fat somewhere close to the 24 percent level, I was concerned enough to make some personal changes in my life-style. I began by walking and, as my conditioning improved, went to slow jogging for long distances. In less than a year I had dropped below 190 pounds and below 20 percent of body fat. After nine years of aerobic exercising, I am at 175 pounds with a body-fat percentage of 15 percent, which I consider ideal for me.

Your rate of progress may be faster or slower than mine. That is not important. What is important is that you commit yourself to getting rid of your extra flab and that you continue to work at it with regular aerobic exercise and sensible eating.

At Oral Roberts University our definition of "obesity level" is 24 percent body fat for males and 34 percent body fat for females. People above these body-fat percentages are usually anywhere from 30 to 100 or more pounds "overweight." I put quotes around the word *overweight* because I am referring to the height/weight tables, which most people understand and use as a frame of reference. We could call that gray area between the ideals (11 to 17 percent for males and 17 to 22 for females) and the obesity levels "somewhat" or "just a little" overfat.

As I said earlier, the height/weight tables are not really accurate. Your fat percentage is what counts, not your weight. With most people, of course, their weight goes down as their fat percentage drops. Because getting weighed underwater or measured with calipers for fat content is not convenient on a daily basis, we use loss of pounds as a rule of thumb in our programs at Oral Roberts University. We require obesity-level students to lose eight pounds (and 1 percent body fat) during each sixteen-week semester. This translates into one-half pound per week, which is not a great deal to ask of anyone.

As you get into your own program you can probably do a lot better than a half a pound a week. How much better should you try to do? Dropping as much as two pounds a week on the average, with variation from week to week, is the *most* that you should expect to lose in a program that is serious but sensible. For someone at obesity level, a loss of one pound per week, or about fifty pounds per year, is an excellent success story. Furthermore, if you lose from one-half to two pounds per week consistently with aerobic activity, it will be a permanent and genuine loss of fat. Fat will not return, but will be gone for good as long as you are faithful in aerobic-exercise activities.

In this book it may sound as though I were the one doing the day-to-day work with the overfat students. In reality my job is as advisor and consultant. During the last school year 100 ORU students were in the overfat group that we call the exercise and weight-control class. Through moderate regular exercise activities the miraculous result was that 91 of that 100 were successful! Credit for this fabulous record goes to the motivation of the students themselves, but Mrs. Sally Schollmeier, the faculty member who teaches, encourages, and leads this exercise and weight-control group, deserves much applause. We need each other.

Greg is a perfect example of how all this can work. A student at ORU, he entered our Health, Physical Education, and Recreation Program at the start of fall term at 313 pounds and body fat of 40 percent. Greg began with walking exercises four times a week. We also gave him plenty of individual counseling and carefully monitored his diet. His cooperation level was excellent.

Greg's enthusiasm mounted with each week. By Christmas his weight had dropped to 282 pounds, and his body fat was at 32.2 percent. By the end of the school year his body fat was 26.7 percent, and his weight was 265.

When Greg started the program, his dimensions included a fifty-inch waist and a twenty-and-a-half-inch collar. At year's end he bought a pair of slacks with a forty-inch waist, and his collar size was down to seventeen. He told us, "For the first time in my life, I've been able to buy clothes off the rack."

Greg's stress level dropped dramatically as well. His

blood pressure went to 140 over 60. When he started the program, he was in a decidedly unhealthy range of 150 over 100.

Through our counseling, Greg discovered he was using food as a weapon to "get back at people." He began eating less at meals and cut out his between-meals snacks, which had featured frequent binges on sweets. At year's end he still had more fat and weight to lose, but he was well on his way and committed to a new life-style. His comment: "I control the eating, it doesn't control me. It's freedom."

You may have noted that Greg lost a total of forty-eight pounds over a school year of nine months. Most important, his body fat went from 40 percent to 26.7 percent. I mentioned that he began the program by walking, something we strongly advised due to his 313 pounds. After a few months he switched to slow jogging, and by year's end was doing thirty to sixty minutes of slow jogging four or five times a week.

Greg is a good model for anyone at severe obesity level to follow. Begin your aerobics with walking and aim for a weight loss of fifty pounds the first year. As you get into better condition, you can switch to jogging, biking, or other activities.

For most people, walking is usually fun to at least some degree, but I often get questions from joggers such as, "When does jogging or running start becoming fun?" I believe many people have been misled by those of us who are promoting exercise. The truth is *not every single minute of every workout is fun.*

My good friend Dr. Thaddeus Kostrubala is a San Diego psychiatrist who wrote the fine book *The Joy of Running.* But Tad was not entirely in agreement with his publishers when they gave his book that title. He says, "I thought the title would mislead people. If you approach running or any other fitness exercise with the idea that it always has to be fun, you are bound to be disappointed. Running is work. Painful work, *glorious* painful work, but it's still work."

Hal Higdon states, "The so-called runner's high may not exist for many people. The fun may come not during exercise, but afterwards, knowing that you are physically fit and more capable of coping with the stress of everyday life."[1]

My own experience is that a mildly vigorous jog becomes fun after the first two miles. If my time schedule permits a longer workout, slow jogging of five, six, or eight miles always proves to be fun during the last half. On days when I take only a shorter jog of maybe two to two-and-a-half miles, it's mostly work, and the joy comes during and after my shower, when I really feel good. For me the shorter workout is seldom fun, but it pays dividends in how good I feel about life afterward.

Keep in mind, however, that this is *not* a book on the joys of jogging or "reaching the runner's high." This is a book about losing fat through aerobic exercise and sensible eating habits. Jogging and running are only two forms of aerobic exercise. You may prefer biking, swimming, or walking, all of which are easier on the feet, knees, and other joints, while still giving you the heart rate you need to reach aerobic-activity levels.

As I have said several times, walking is something almost anyone can do. A brisk walk is usually enjoyable from the first step. That is not to say walking won't get you tired or that there won't be days when a brisk walk doesn't look half as enticing as a slow amble to the TV recliner. Those are the days when you will have to decide whether you want to be fit or fat.

No, aerobic exercise is not quick and it is not easy, but it can be tremendously rewarding. You can achieve the weight you want. You can rid yourself of those extra layers of unlovely fat by committing yourself to a lifetime of aerobic exercise and sensible eating.

I have mentioned "sensible eating" at several points. Maybe it's time we took a brief look at what sensible eating is all about.

10

Why You Should Eat Smart, Not Less

In a book like this it is easy to emphasize exercise to the point that it sounds as though it doesn't matter what or how much you eat. But that would be foolish. As chapter one stressed, exercise is the horse and diet is the cart. Exercise comes *first*, but diet has to be there also or you do not have a complete approach to fighting flab correctly.

I do have trouble, however, with that word *diet*. I'd like to throw the term *diet* out the window and promote the concept of "eating smart." We have preached diets and dieting so hard in our culture that the word has come to have mostly negative connotations. Mention the word *diet* around your friends or acquaintances and you do not see any smiles of joy and happiness. I've yet to see a book titled *The High of Dieting*. Eating sensibly sounds much more positive. To eat sensibly is a happy experience in every way, socially as well as psychologically and physiologically.

To talk about eating sensibly, we have to look at the various food groups and how much or how little we should have of each main group. You may be familiar with some of what follows, but I think it's important to go over it as review to show just how your eating habits should tie in with your exercise activities.

We have already mentioned the three major groupings of food: fats, carbohydrates, and protein. In a book on getting rid of fat it will come as no surprise that a good rule is to eat less fat. Americans eat an average of 42 percent of their daily calories in fatty foods, but the recommended amount is 30 percent. With a little effort you can easily identify most of the fatty foods. Fat intake slips up on us when we least expect it; it is found in food more than we think.

For example, butter and margarine are almost 100 percent fat, and both are used extensively in cooking. Another source of fat is meat. We think we are getting "pure" protein in steaks and high-quality ground beef. But in these types of meat, the more expensive cuts are usually the highest in fat. It's all right to eat steak or ground beef, but use small portions, especially of the marbled varieties that are streaked with fat for better taste.

You may have heard that, along with cutting down on fats, it's wise to go easy on the carbohydrates. Entire diets have been built around the cutting of carbohydrates to very low levels. An example of this type of diet is found in *Dr. Atkins' Diet Revolution.*[1] I believe carbohydrates have received unmerited "bad press" for years. It's true that we need to reduce our use of *refined carbohydrates*, like sugar and white flour, because they are high in calories and extremely low in nutritional value. But we need to *increase* our use of *complex carbohydrates*, which provide energy, fiber, vitamins, and minerals. Excellent sources of complex carbohydrates are vegetables, whole-grain breads and cereals, and fresh fruit.

Foods with complex carbohydrates provide a double bonus: (1) Many of them contain fiber, which helps with digestion and keeping the colon clear; and (2) some of these foods are quite low in calories.

Personally, I tossed out my calorie-counter books years ago, because I depend so directly on aerobic exercise for fat-and-weight control. Nonetheless, I realize many people are calorie conscious or try to be. So, early in your own fat-loss program, you may need to keep an eye on your calorie intake. After all, if you are trying to lose fat and want to burn more calories than you're taking in, why have a high-calorie dish when something else, with less than half the number of calories, is available?

For example, in the complex-carbohydrate family many vegetables like green beans, cauliflower, broccoli, and carrots are very low in calories. Be careful, however, with avocados (which are quite high in calories), and some of the fruits. For example, bananas, prunes, and raisins are "calorie dynamite." All these are good, but go easy.

Sometimes the calorie count rises according to how a food is prepared. Potatoes are often labeled as high in calories, but actually a medium-sized potato contains zero fat and about 125 calories. Turn that potato into French fries, however, and you can increase the fat content to 65 percent, and the calorie count jumps to several hundred.

Carbohydrates are quite likely the most misunderstood food group of all. A lot of people think they have to reduce carbohydrate intake, but in most cases people need to *increase* carbohydrate consumption to around 50 to 60 percent of their daily total. Just be sure you are getting the "good guys"—the complex carbohydrates I mentioned above.

Protein might be called the "glamour" food group. Protein is advertised as vitally important to the body and this is true, because it is the source of essential amino acids that are necessary for the building and maintenance of body cells and functions.

Good sources of protein are fish, poultry, and legumes. Three other high-protein sources are red meat, eggs, and cheese, but try to go easy on these. As I have already mentioned, red meat can be very high in fat; eggs and cheese increase cholesterol. Actually, in America we have an overabundance of good-quality protein. For the typical American family, protein intake of 12 percent of total calories is sufficient. Protein also comes in vegetables in the legume family—peas, dried beans, and lentils.

There is much debate about minerals and vitamins, and the subject is too broad to tackle in a brief book on how to lose fat. If you are interested in learning more, you can read about them in any number of good books that are available at health-food stores or your local bookshop. We do not have to get into the fine points of argument to realize that our bodies need all of the essential vitamins and minerals. I am not at all sure that the recommended daily allowances (RDA) are really enough, however, for persons exercising vigorously and regularly in an aerobic program. So, for instance, I take a simple multiple vitamin-and-mineral supplement. I also take moderate extra doses of vitamins C, E, and B complex. Whenever I get muscle aches, I also take some calcium.

There are physicians who may tell you that if you eat a well-balanced general diet, you will need no extra vitamins or minerals. No one really knows if this is right or wrong. As more and more data continue to come in, we are getting a better picture. But until all the evidence is gathered, why not be sure? A multiple vitamin-and-mineral supplement is a small investment in good nutritional insurance.

Be careful, however, not to overdose on vitamins, particularly vitamins C, A, D, and E. I recently treated a runner who had severe urinary bleeding until I convinced him to cut down from ten grams of vitamin C each day to one-half gram per day.

We have taken a look at the three basic food types: fats, carbohydrates, and protein. In order to get the balance and variety that is so important to your total diet, I suggest that you follow what is called the Four Basic Food

Groups Plan. In these four basic food groups you can find
adequate amounts of fat, carbohydrates, and protein.

The first group is the meat group, which provides proteins, minerals, fats, and B vitamins. Included here are red
meats, fish, poultry, dried peas, beans, lentils, peanut butter, and nuts. There is a lot of talk today about the dangers
of eating a great deal of red meat. Being an Oklahoman, I
may get some calls from my friends in the cattle business,
but I have to recommend cutting down on red meat. I have
already covered the problems with "marbled steak,"
which is streaked with fat. Many people are switching to
more fish and poultry instead of having their usual ham-
burgers, roast beef, steak, pork roast, and so forth. My own
eating habits have changed over the last few years, and I
now have beef only once or twice a week, while fish and
chicken and some vegetarian meals have become staples in
my diet.

The second major food group is fruit and vegetables, of
which you should have four servings each day. Here is
where you get vitamins A and C, minerals, and fiber. Included are foods like citrus fruits, melons, tomatoes, straw-
berries, broccoli, carrots, leafy greens, squashes, potatoes,
and yams. As you pick from this group, be sure you include
one green or yellow vegetable per day and one citrus fruit
or medium-sized glass of citrus juice such as orange or
grapefruit juice.

The third group is bread and cereal, and you should
eat four servings of these daily. Here's where you get carbohydrates, proteins, vitamins, and minerals. If you choose
"natural cereals" like granola, oatmeal, cornmeal, and
"seven grain" mixtures, you will get some of your requirement of fiber, which is so important to keeping your digestive tract clear. Try to get all the fiber you can. Another
thing in its favor is that fiber fills you up without filling you
out.

Still another excellent source of fiber is 100 percent
whole wheat bread, particularly brands with bran added.
Other good natural breads include those containing rye or

rice. Go easy on the highly advertised "junk food" cereals. They have very little nutritional value and are loaded with sugar.

The fourth group is dairy products, which provide calcium, phosphorus, proteins, vitamin A, and riboflavin (a B vitamin). Included in the milk or dairy-product group are milk, yogurt, cheese, and ice cream. You should have two or more servings of this group daily. Watch the dairy-product group carefully, however, to keep your fat intake down. You can control fat intake by drinking only nonfat milk and using low-calorie yogurt, or skim-milk cheese. Stay away from ice cream except for occasional splurges to give yourself a treat for normally being self-disciplined.

Don't think that fat is a problem only in the milk or dairy-product group. Watch all of the four groups for too much fat. Avoid high-calorie baked goods, deep-fried foods, cream products, solid fats, sauces, and gravies.

In the above paragraphs I have given only the barest sketch of the three basic food types (fats, carbohydrates, and proteins) and the four basic food groups (meat, fruit and vegetable, bread and cereal, milk and dairy products). If you want to learn more, I suggest that you pick up one or more diet or nutrition books and do a little reading to become familiar with what you are consuming daily in each basic food group and food type.[2] You will also quickly become an "expert" on calories and which foods have high-calorie and low-calorie counts.

Calories do count and they count up fast, especially when you eat fatty foods. Each of us has to work out his own eating plan to get the right amount of each food type and group, enough vitamins and minerals, and yet keep the daily calorie intake within reasonable levels. All of this is part of eating smart, or sensibly.

Please, however, do not always nitpick about the number of calories you are eating. Just keep in mind that if you want to indulge yourself, it means that you need to do a little more walking or jogging to burn off the extra calories that the indulgence has added. My personal nemesis is the pie counter. I confess that my indiscretion occurs quite often, and I am well aware that I must burn an extra 300 or 400 calories on the jogging path every time I down a piece of pie.

Please understand that I am not giving you license to commit this kind of folly as regularly as I do. If you are engaging faithfully in enough aerobic activity, however, you can work out your own system for having an occasional treat. The point is if you are having your daily walk or run or bike ride and eating sensibly, you do not have to worry about every calorie you consume. An occasional treat is easy to handle, but let me emphasize the word *occasional*. If you start gobbling up all the pie, cake, and ice cream in sight, while trying to mix in a little aerobic activity and a half-hearted attempt to eat sensibly, you are headed for disaster, and the fat will go right back on your body. If you are in any kind of weight and fat-loss program, you should eat at least 1200 calories per day with a very balanced selection of foods.

If you start talking about nutrition and calories, some of your friends and acquaintances may start to kid you or even start to get irritated with your remarks. Don't be obnoxious, but at the same time don't back off out of embarrassment or timidity. Today, nutrition is recognized as an absolutely vital element in health care. In the Surgeon General's 1979 report on health promotion and disease prevention, entitled "Healthy People," the following suggestions were made concerning nutrition. Americans would be healthier as a whole if they consumed: (1) only sufficient calories to meet body needs and maintain desirable weight; (2) less saturated fat and cholesterol; (3) less salt; (4) less sugar; (5) relatively more complex carbohydrates such as whole grains, cereals, fruits, and vegetables; (6) relatively more fish, poultry, and legumes and less red meat.

In summary, there are three simple rules you can follow:

1.   Cut down on fats. Try to eat only 30 percent of your daily calories in fat. Watch the junk food like French fries and the number of pats of butter that you can sneak into each meal without realizing it. A fairly good balance for a diet would include 30 percent in fats, 55 to 60 percent in complex carbohydrates, and 10 to 15 percent in high-quality protein.

2.   Eat a wide variety of foods (review the material on the four basic food groups). Most people could stand getting acquainted with a great many more fruits and vegetables. As I work with people at our Health Service, my main concyrn is that they use as much natural food as possible without having to go to undue expense at health-food stores. I recommend a "vegetarian type" of diet, with additions of fowl or fish and very little red meat.

3.   Watch your calories but don't carry a calculator to every meal. Get a general idea of the amounts of calories in the basic foods that you like and consume daily and weekly. Then eat only the sufficient number of calories you need to keep up your strength and your aerobic activities.

All three of the above rules can be condensed into one: *Eat a good nutritional diet.* Don't waste your time on empty calories. As long as you are out there trying to burn away that fat with aerobic exercise, you might as well be filling your tank with the right fuel.

Yes, it's a little more trouble to watch what you eat and to be aware of food groups and food types, but it's more than worth it. Along with committing yourself to a life-style that includes aerobic exercise, commit yourself to a life-style that includes proper eating habits. And when I use the word *commit,* I am talking about saying, *"I will do this,"* not "I guess I'll try." The fight against flab is waged on the exercise track and at the table, but you win it or lose it in your head. For some tips on waging successful psychological warfare, see the next chapter.

11

You Really Are What You Think!

"Attitude Decreases Fattitude" could be another title for this chapter. One counselor told me that two out of three persons who come to him have as their major problem inadequate self-esteem. Repeatedly, he sees living proof of the old saying: "You become or remain what you think you are."

The concept of "you are what you think" has obvious implications for fat people. Your layers of flab are *not* the real you, but if you think you can't lose and that you'll "just have to live with being heavy," you will be trapped in a fat body and quite likely suffer from low self-esteem.

But it doesn't have to be so. *Anyone who is able to walk does not have to be fat.* You can be sure that God doesn't make junk, and he does not want his beautiful creation enfolded in excess flab.

So, think thin! Move out slowly but surely into an active life-style. Keep visualizing the slender you that you want to become. Stick with it and you will become thin. Remember that you are someone special. You can achieve whatever your mind conceives—*if you really want to.*

The power of what the mind can do is illustrated in the story of Lois (not her real name, but definitely a real person). A few years ago my wife and I sought to help Lois as she struggled with trying to lose weight and fat. Lois came from a home in which she lived with her mother, grandmother, and aunt. All three of the older women weighed over 200 pounds. Lois' father had deserted the family when she was very young.

Lois' mother, grandmother, and aunt all gave her a great deal of love and attention. How did they express love? You guessed it: with food. Day after day Lois was programmed with one basic concept—caring means feeding.

For Lois to become slender, or even to desire a healthy slim body, she would have to undergo a reprogramming of her attitudes. She had a negative picture of men (due to her father's desertion), and she was totally dominated by the concept that a caring person is an obese woman who prepares and provides rich, fatty foods.

We tried diligently to alter Lois' basic thinking but we failed. Lois finally left school to return to the safe retreat of the all-feminine circle where love was expressed with food. She did not like being fat, but she found security in a situation where she could see herself only as a fat person receiving love from other fat people. Lois simply could not picture herself as thin.

A girl we'll call Denise has a story with a much happier ending. When Denise began our program, she had a kidney problem that required her to be on a dialysis machine two or three times a week. With body fat of 35.4 percent Denise was definitely at obesity level. She stood a good five feet five inches and weighed 200 pounds. Her dress size was eighteen to twenty and she wore size eighteen jeans. As she started her program, which featured aerobic walking exercises, she focused on her clothes

You become or remain what you think you are, so think thin!

and began "picturing" herself in smaller sizes. By the end of the school year she was in a size eleven-twelve dress and her "Jordache look" was a size thirteen! Her body fat went down to 27.5 percent, and her weight dropped to 176 pounds. Even more important, she was able to decrease her visits to the kidney dialysis machine from two to three times a week to once a month.

Other improvements by Denise included an increase in her self-confidence and ability to relate to others. She showed a marked decrease in worry about what people thought of her and proved this by showing a marked increase in wanting to go to the store to buy clothes.

"I just kept seeing myself as a smaller person," Denise commented. "I prayed I wouldn't have to keep hiding by standing by the wall."

Denise's emotional improvements are typical of people who get into programs of regular exercise. Tom Lee, an R.N. on our ORU staff, recently did some fascinating research concerning the effect of aerobic exercise on depression. At the beginning of the fall term, he used the Taylor Johnson Temperament Analysis to test forty-four freshmen women who had never engaged in any form of continuing physical exercise. After taking the test, all of the women engaged in a gradually increasing exercise program of the same type that all first-year students are asked to follow at Oral Roberts University.

After six to nine months the women were brought back for retesting with the Taylor Johnson Temperament Analysis. All of the women who showed marked depression in their first TJTA test were significantly improved when retested.

The key to ridding yourself of depression or other negative emotional states like anxiety, worry, hostility, and so forth is to realize you are a very special person. As self-esteem goes up, problems like depression have to come down. One psychological tool that I often use with people trying to lose weight and fat is the idea of positive reward. Once you are into an aerobic exercise program and losing one to three pounds every week, you start to feel good about yourself. You know you are losing actual fat, because your clothes are fitting better or possibly even becoming a bit too large for you. Inches are melting away slowly but surely. That is the time to reward yourself by buying a new dress or perhaps a color-coordinated jogging outfit. (I always caution people not to buy the most expensive items, because they may be trimming away even more inches, and what they purchase may eventually become too big also.)

Of course there are many ways to reward yourself other than buying yourself something. Perhaps you can change the route for your aerobic workouts. Walk along the river or in the park instead of along the same old path through the neighborhood.

·Reward yourself by switching to bicycling or roller skating instead of jogging each day. Boredom is a dangerous enemy of the person who has achieved some success in an aerobic program. Change the scenery or the type of activity and it will help with boredom.

Another kind of reward that I find most pleasant is taking a day to go fishing or backpacking. With backpacking, aerobic activity is built right into the enjoyment. Even fishing can be aerobic if there is a canoe to paddle or a boat to row.

Another thing you might want to do is skip a day of aerobics, or even two days (but absolutely no more than that). In the end, it will be a slight change in the routine, and you can take a couple of days just to relax and feel proud of yourself. Don't be surprised, however, if you are restless and anxious to get back on the jogging or walking trail. Once the aerobic exercise bug bites you, you find it difficult to stay away from exercise, and you feel "antsy" or sluggish if you don't get in your daily workout.

Another way to reward yourself is in what you eat. Perhaps you enjoy between-meal snacks. Indulge yourself, but as I said in an earlier chapter, *eat smart!* Try whole wheat crackers and skim-milk cheese, or learn the realistic delights of carrot sticks or celery. The best approach to losing flab is to eat five or six *small* meals per day anyway. Just be aware of how many calories you are consuming, and keep your consumption of fats well under control. Have a between-meals snack now and then, but don't go off the deep end with continual munching and feeling justified by saying, "Well, I'm going to get in my workout later, so I can handle this."

If you are confident you can handle it, use dessert as a rare reward. From time to time have a dish of ice cream or a piece of pie. Just be sure that you really desire the dessert treat. Never eat a dessert you don't really want.

Remember that when you use desserts as a rare reward, the emphasis is on the word *rare*. You can't make desserts a twice-daily habit and expect to get much results. An occasional dessert will give you fat and carbohydrates that you can burn in your aerobic program. It's true that most Americans need to cut down on fat and sugar, but you don't have to cut them out completely if you are exercising regularly. Americans consume an average of 125 pounds of sugar per person per year, an almost obscene figure. There is no reason, however, why you can't handle sixty pounds per year, *if you are burning it off with aerobics*. Try to stay away from the soft drinks, however. They are a highly concentrated form of sugar that isn't good for anyone, even the most dedicated aerobics participant.

As you can see, there are many ways to "think yourself thin." Don't fail to use the psychology of positive reinforcement whenever and wherever you can. In whatever you do, use thought patterns and rewards that are meaningful to *you*. As the hair-color commercial puts it, "You're worth it!"

12

The Power of Setting Goals

While it's true that you are, or you become, what you think, it's equally true that you have to do more than simply envision yourself as a slender person. The other side of the thinking-thin coin is to set some goals and plan how you are actually going to become thin.

I always urge people in our weight-loss programs at ORU to set *long-term goals* and to have some intermediate expectations or subgoals that they can reach along the way. For example, losing fifty pounds in one year is an excellent goal for someone who is truly obese. For others, losing anywhere from ten to twenty pounds in a year would be a very realistic goal for one year's time.

Whatever you do, don't ever plan to lose more than two pounds a week. True, you may go into a program of dieting and exercise and suddenly drop several pounds in a few days. Much of this is water, and there will be no harm in this faster weight loss early in the program.

After you lose a few pounds, you usually reach a plateau where it becomes more difficult. For some weeks you might not drop another ounce. If there were some easy, quick way to measure flab daily, you could see that you are losing fat even though your weight remains unchanged. Remember that even when you aren't losing pounds, you are burning off fat if you are faithfully engaging in sufficient aerobic exercise and eating sensibly. And it's fat that you want to get rid of.

Your ultimate goal should be losing what jiggles and bulges where it's not supposed to. Another goal might be to lose a dress size or a couple of inches on belt size. Whatever goal you set, be realistic.

At the ORU Health Service we work hard to help everyone set realistic goals. Our fat-control program is positive, effective, and popular for the most part. An overwhelming majority of those who have participated have been helped toward a new life-style that is healthy and slender.

As I mentioned in chapter nine, our standards classify obesity level at 24 percent fat for male students and 34 percent fat for females. People at obesity levels are placed in special exercise and weight-control classes. Their goal is to lose eight pounds and at least 1 percent of body fat during a sixteen-week semester, an average loss of one-half pound per week. We have found that almost anyone can reach these goals if he or she is not bound or hampered by other problems.

Of course many students exceed the loss of eight pounds per semester. Some have dropped as much as twenty and thirty pounds during one semester. We always ask students to be careful over Christmas and summer vacations. These are critical periods to guard against regaining any of their lost weight and fat. Then they are asked to lose another eight pounds and additional percentages of body fat during the next semester. This routine continues until the students reach levels of fat percentage that are termed "below obesity."

A girl I will call Tina is a good example of someone who made excellent progress over the year. While she didn't lose quite as much body-fat percentage as needed, she did drop in weight according to her goals, and she held that figure through those critical Christmas vacation and summer vacation times. Tina came into our program at 44.5 percent body fat and at a weight of 209 pounds. By Christmas she had dropped to 42.1 percent body fat and she weighed 196. By year's end her weight was at 191—a total loss of 18 pounds over the year—and her body fat was at 39.6 percent. She held those numbers over the summer and came back the next fall to continue working hard in the program with new resolve to reach her coveted body-fat-percentage level of under 34 percent.

Obviously most of the readers of this book will not have the benefit of the Oral Roberts University HPER weight-loss program. You're probably going to have to do it on your own. If you have no significant physical problems (other than excess flab), here is an outline of how to proceed. You can plug into the following steps at any point, depending on how much weight and fat you need to lose:

1.   If you are in the "high obesity" range (anywhere from 50 to 100 pounds or more overweight), make your goal the loss of 50 pounds per year until you reach a level below 34 percent body fat (women) or below 24 percent body fat (men). You will, of course have to establish your body-fat percentage to begin with. You can do this with underwater weighing or some form of skin-fold estimate (see chapter three).

2.   Once you drop out of high-obesity range (above 34 percent body fat for women and 24 percent body fat for men) you are in what I call "low obesity" level or "over-fat." Your fat percentage will be around 20 to 24 percent for men and 30 to 34 percent for women. You will still want to work on losing fat and weight and at this level a

loss of twenty pounds per year is realistic. Your body-fat percentage will drop accordingly.

3.   As you drop below 20 percent body-fat percentage for men or 30 percent body-fat percentage for women, you are approaching your final goal. You will recall that in chapter three I gave a range of "ideal body-fat percentages": 11 to 17 percent for men and 17 to 22 percent for women. As you work toward your ideal weight and percentage of body fat you should aim for a loss of around ten pounds per year. At this stage don't be in a hurry; your body will be in much better condition and will be taking its time about losing those last pounds and percentages. Shoot for a slow, steady decrease in skin-fold thickness over several years of time.

One more word about measuring percentages of body fat: At the ORU Health Service we have found that the only accurate way to measure people in high-obesity levels is with underwater weighing. Skin-fold calipers just aren't reliable because in a highly obese person the skin is pulled too tight to allow for the correct amount of "pinching" of the skin. Once you are in the low-obesity range, however, calipers do the job quite well. You may get so interested in your new "flabless" life-style that you will want to buy your own set of calipers. On the other hand, you may be content to get measured by your physician, or at a local Y or fitness center.

As you set your goals and work toward them, remember one thing: Losing fat permanently is a slow and steady process. Put out of your mind forever the psychology and reasoning of people who push crash diets, losing a few pounds in order to get into next summer's swimsuit, and so forth. If you try to lose fat rapidly, you may succeed temporarily, but it will just come back, usually worse than before.

By faithful use of aerobic exercise, you can reach your "perfect" fat and weight levels. *Once you are there, however, don't stop your aerobic-exercise program.* If you do, all your work will be lost and the flab will return. You will have to maintain workouts at least three or four times a week to stay at the level where you want to be.

Sincere flab fighters are sentenced to life on the aerobic road. You can walk it, jog it, run it, bike it, or swim it, but you *can never get off.* Interestingly enough, you won't want to. You'll be hooked on being thin, happy—and healthy!

13

Why Walking Is a "Perfect" Exercise

Up to this point I have emphasized over and over that engaging in aerobic exercise *does not* mean that you have to become a world-class Olympic athlete. Many people equate aerobics with jogging or running, covering three to ten miles a day at brisk paces like eight minutes per mile, or less. We read constantly of marathons (a distance of over twenty-six miles) or "ten K" runs (approximately six miles). All of this is there for you only if you get into great condition and want to participate. If running or jogging is not your bag, however, you can always walk your way to victory over flab.

As my good friend Charlie emphasizes, the key is not outstanding athletic accomplishment; the key is learning to be active at a pace that is pleasant and easy for you. Charlie's full name is Dr. Charles T. Kuntzleman, and he is one of the leading health and fitness experts in the country today. While an executive at the national level in the

YMCA, Charlie has developed three national YMCA fitness programs. He has also written more than a dozen books on health and fitness along with conducting over 100 fitness and weight-loss workshops across the United States and Canada during the last few years. He is a national director of Living Well, Inc.

In one of his books, *Your Active Way to Weight Control*, Charlie makes some excellent suggestions for developing an active life-style that will result in a slender, healthful you. One of his chapters is titled, "Walking, the Perfect Exercise." Here he quotes a study by Dr. Michael Pollock of Mount Sinai Hospital, Milwaukee, Wisconsin. Dr. Pollock used a group of healthy, yet sedentary, men between the ages of forty and fifty-six. After twenty weeks of walking two and one-half to three miles a day, at least four days a week, the transformation in the physical condition of these middle-aged men was fantastic. Following is a lengthy excerpt from Charlie's book that gives you his reasoning and enthusiastic endorsement for walking as an aerobic exercise:

> Naturally, for walking to be aerobic, you need to "walk with authority." If you shuffle a few steps, stop and smell the roses, and then shuffle a few more, it probably won't increase your heart rate more than ten beats. Instead, step out. Swing your arms. Hold your head up high and walk with pride. Move just fast enough to make you breathe deeply. You will soon discover walking can keep you at your target heart rate, burning those calories and fat away.
>
> It's safe. Unlike most recreational sports there is no one to bump into, no fast ball to dodge, no tackler to avoid, no apparatus to fall from, and no barbell to drop on your toes. When you leave your house for a walk, you are engaging in a safe, yet healthy, exercise. Walking is an exercise that spans all age groups. It is a great exercise to do together. What better way to enjoy fitness than as a family.

Remember, the key to any exercise, including walking is your pulse rate and personal feeling. Your walk should also be painless. If you experience any chest pain, jaw, or neck pain, slow down. If that doesn't stop the pain, see your doctor and describe what happened.

The minimum of twenty minutes is recommended. Six days per week is your ultimate goal. If you take more than two days off, you will lose the benefits from your walking program.

Build walking into your life. Here's where the fun comes. And creativity. As you begin to examine your lifestyle, you will find innumerable ways to program more activity into your daily routine. You can turn those idle moments into pleasurable, fat-burning walking. Here are some suggestions:

1) Never drive less than one mile. Think of the number of trips you make that are less than one mile, to church, to the post office, to school. Make a pact with yourself, that from this day forward I will walk instead of drive whenever the trip is less than a mile. You will save gas and burn a few calories with each trip.

2) Park in the good spots. You may need to reconsider what good means. The really good parking spots are the ones that no one else wants, farthest away from the entrance to the store, factory, or office, but you never have to fight to get one. You can pull into your spot, get out, and take a brisk walk to your destination and still probably get there faster than the people driving around in circles looking for a spot up front.

3) Have a walking lunch. Instead of standing in line at the fast food counter or waiting in a crowded restaurant for the waitress to bring you your order, carry a whole wheat sandwich and some fruit, or a thermos of soup, and walk to a park bench. Enjoy your lunch. Then spend the remainder of your lunch break walking. Great nutrition and great exercise.

4) Take a short walk just before supper. The usual rou-

tine for a person who works is to walk through the door, grab the newspaper and a drink, then sit down until dinner. This type of break, however, is hazardous for the health-conscious. Drinking a beer or a mixed drink increases calories and elevates your appetite. Consequently, you end up eating more for supper and feel like doing nothing more than returning to the easy chair and an evening of television. The end result is an evening of sitting and eating. A pleasant ten- or fifteen-minute walk can be effective in reducing the job tension from your day, and often exercise tends to curb your appetite. In the end you win out by dealing with tension and fatigue in a positive way, probably consuming fewer calories, and getting in a little extra walking.

5)   Avoid elevators and escalators. It sounds simple, but in exercise every little bit helps. Besides, you usually get there quicker this way since there are no waiting lines.

Walking may not be perfect, but it's the closest to perfect as an exercise suited for anyone, anytime, and any place. It burns up calories to help you lose weight and it produces positive changes in your cardiovascular system, and walking is as close as your front door.[1]

While I'm a jogger myself, I agree completely with everything Charlie says in the above paragraphs. He makes a convincing case for walking as the "perfect" approach to aerobic exercise. Even though I jog long distances for the most part, I still do a great deal of walking as well. Furthermore, I see additional living proof of the benefits of walking in Peggy, who is now a nurse on our department staff at ORU. You might say she walked her way into the job.

Peggy came to school to work on a B.S. degree in nursing. Because she was at 35.5 percent body fat and 178 pounds, she got into our program to reduce high-level obesity. By year's end she was down to 166 pounds, a bit short of our goal of eight pounds per semester. But her body-fat percentage was down to 28 percent, which was excellent progress.

The change in Peggy's self-image and confidence level was also extremely noticeable. I believe it is safe to say that she never would have had the courage to ask for a job in our department if she hadn't participated in the aerobic program.

She continues to work on her weight and fat percentage. I see her every day at work, of course, but more encouraging is seeing her after hours walking up a storm on our track for thirty to sixty minutes five or six times a week. She's looking better all the time.

Walking does work. My suggestion is to get out there and try it. Most of us had to crawl before we could walk. Many of us need to walk before we jog or run. The good news is that walking is all we need. So, go for a walk—right now!

14

What Do Other Experts Say?

My studies and research in the field of nutrition and weight/fat control have turned up some excellent material that I hate to leave out of a book on fighting flab successfully. The following are comments by two men I respect highly. Some of what they say underlines what I've said in earlier chapters; a great deal of what they say expands on and enlarges the basic subject of obesity and what you can do about it.

Dr. Jean Mayer has done some of the most outstanding work in this country in the field of nutrition and obesity. In an interview published in *Life and Health*, he was asked, "Just what is obesity?" Here is his reply:

A well-trained athlete in excellent physical shape may weigh more than the average person, and hence, be overweight. But his extra weight is muscle and he is not obese. Another man may have the same height and weight, but be obese because he is loaded with excessive fat.

The easiest way and most obvious way to tell whether you are obese is to look at yourself naked in the mirror. If you look fat you probably are fat. Then it is fairly easy to estimate the amount of fat by pinching your skin and underlying fat between your thumb and first finger. The best place is the back of the upper arm. If this fold of skin and fat is much greater than an inch, you are excessively fat. For men, there is another simple test. If your belt line is longer than the circumference of your chest at the nipples, you have too much abdominal fat.

As to the cause of obesity, these are related to one's body build, hormone balance, heredity and *activity*. The major factor is not hormones or heredity or glucose receptors, but physical inactivity. If your activity goes up we find that your food intake tends to go *down* a little bit. It certainly doesn't increase.

We can encourage people to lose weight simply by having them exercise more. We have programs in which we have reduced the weight of hundreds of children without touching their food intake, simply by increasing their physical activity.

We did studies on obese and nonobese children during exercise by taking motion pictures of these children. Even during these sports, the nonobese children were much more active than the obese, and when we consider the actual energy they were using, the obese were burning up less than the nonobese.

We found in another experiment that fat babies eat small to moderate amounts, but were very sluggish. Extremely thin babies eat large amounts of food, but were very active.

There is a difference between things that are tiring and things that are exercise. That's something that people don't understand. Doing housework may be tiring and boring, but it is not necessarily a lot of exercise. It may use far less energy than going window shopping when you walk there and walk back, even though the latter is relaxing.

What about those who don't eat very much, maybe 500 to 600 calories a day, and still don't lose? They may not lose over a short-term basis because some people replace lost fat with water. But if people are on 600 calories a day, they'll lose weight, eventually.

I believe that obesity is largely determined by genetic traits. The environment in which one lives is uniformly favorable to the development of obesity. If you have the wrong gene, you will get fat unless you take specific measures to avoid it. But if you are willing to fight the battle on a consistent basis, you do not have to be fat, even if you do have the fat genes.

My suggestions for weight loss are nothing very original. Cut down on calories, which means, basically, I would practically eliminate sugar and cut down on fats, particularly saturated fats. I think that it is good to cut out the junk foods. Do not cut down on major foods, but on soft drinks, a lot of snack foods, and any food high in fat. I do eat more salads, fruits, and vegetables, fish and whole-grain cereals. It is important to learn something about the caloric value of food. People think they know, but make grave mistakes on this basis.

Portion size is all-important. The amount of a food that is permitted is a major portion of the prescription. Another factor to remember is that the mode of preparation has a great deal to do with its caloric content. A potato may contain only 100 calories, but when it is made into French fries or hash browns in bacon fat you can build it up to 400 to 500 calories, but it is still potatoes.

Finally, I think that more exercise on a daily basis, starting with walking and habitually practicing it, is *essential*.[1]

Another nutrition authority is George B. Mann, a medical doctor who is an associate professor of medicine and biochemistry at Vanderbilt University. Dr. Mann also was interviewed by the *Life and Health* journal and he states:

In spite of the wide use and even wider acceptance of height/weight tables as indicators of obesity, no real basis for such classification has ever been made and we have no objective, reliable method by which to judge frame size, small, large, or medium, as these tables do.

Taking advantage of the opportunity offered by the height/weight tables, certain segments of industry have systematically exploited obesity as a profitable device. The real culprit, in my opinion, is the food industry. I use this term loosely because I must include in it some marginal soft drink promoters, the pharmaceutical industry which makes millions with ineffectual appetite-control drug promotion, and the clothing industry, that in quite fickle and arbitrary ways tells women, especially younger ones, how they should look.

Why do people become fat? First, we can dispel some myths. Genetic or hereditary causes in human beings are of minor importance. We are left with the inescapable fact that fat people are calorically unbalanced because they are not physically active enough. They tend to be slothful, and if this sloth is associated with overeating, so easy in this era of the auto, the subway, and the supermarket, obesity becomes the state of the majority. The treatment is obvious: go to work.

Fewer than five percent of obese people successfully lose weight by dietary restrictions. We have a higher cure rate for cancer and no one has shown that health has been measurably improved by these dietary methods, although it is easy to show that health has often been harmed by them. The worst offenders in this business are the soft drink producers and the processed breakfast cereal promoters.

Careful studies show that the amphetamines do not effectively control obesity. It is profitable to worry people about fatness and to sell them ineffectual treatments.

Young women, starving themselves, produce two new health hazards. One, deficient iron intake on these low-energy diets produces the very changes of skin and hair which they most abhor—prematurely aged skin. The other consequence is that undernourished mothers have premature, underweight, low-iron babies that are poor risks for survival. We pay a big price for our fashion-plate figures.

TOPS and Weight Watchers do better than the doctors, but I think that they do it the hard way by over-restricting variety and depriving themselves of certain foods that would be wholesome if used judiciously. My method is more liberal. The motto is "Burn it, Baby, Burn it." The doctrine is, be fit and active and you can pretty well eat what you wish.

I conclude with some remarks about how to become fit and how to stay fit. This approach requires you to abandon that Victorian notion that women should never perspire, never go out in the sun, and never seem too muscular. This is all wrong. Women should be vigorous, as indeed they are in thin cultures. The best way to wash your skin is with your own sweat. The best way to restore your figure is to build a muscular support. The best way to regain your iron stores is to eat some good iron-rich food. The best way I know to prevent coronary heart disease is to keep physically fit.

I know from work with other cultures that the lean and handsome people are the active ones who eat generously and would think a person who willfully starves himself or tries to be thin and bony is surely some kind of a nut, and I think they are right.[2]

There's not much to add except to suggest that you might want to print Dr. Mann's motto, "Burn it, Baby, Burn it," in large letters on a card or sheet of paper and paste it on your refrigerator or possibly your bathroom mirror. As you burn off the calories with aerobic exercise, you can eat practically anything you want to (within reason of course) and stay fit and unfat for life!

15

What You Should Know About the "Setpoint Theory"

Ever since chapter one I have been loudly insisting that exercise is the key to losing flab and keeping it lost. A relatively new concept called the "setpoint theory" lends further weight to the case for continued exercise. In their new book, *The Dieter's Dilemma*, Dr. William Bennett and coauthor Joel Gurin describe scientific research that strongly suggests we are all programmed genetically to have a certain level of fatness.[1] This genetically determined internal control system, or "setpoint," originates somewhere in the brain. Your setpoint acts like a sort of thermostat that tells the body how much fat it should carry. Some of us come with a high setting on our "fat thermostats" and others have a lower one. We get that setting at birth; it is the luck of the genetic draw.

As I mentioned in chapter two, we all have our per-

manent number of fat cells by the time we are in late adolescence. The setpoint theory says we inherit that number
of cells and there's nothing we can do about it. Other
theories say we develop our fat cells throughout childhood
and if we overeat as children, we wind up with more and
larger cells than we should. All the scientific evidence is
not in yet, but I believe both theories probably apply. We
are genetically programmed at birth with a "setpoint" of
fat cells. If we overeat as children and as early adolescents,
that setpoint can be raised even higher.

Once the setpoint is established, it is almost impossible to change it through dieting only. The setpoint theory
says that when you go on a diet—particularly a crash diet
with a very low calorie intake—your body rebels. You see,
your body doesn't know the difference between a crash
diet and starving to death. Your setpoint "thermostat"
starts working overtime to do two things:

1.   The setpoint mechanism sends signals to your metabolic system that say in essence, "The body is starving!
Slow down—don't burn the calories so fast."
2.   The setpoint system sends signals to your appetite
control center that say, "You're hungry! Eat more to get
the body back up to its proper level."

While it is still an unproven theory, the setpoint concept provides an excellent explanation for why many—if
not most—people who try to lose fat and weight by dieting
only almost always regain what they lose. Their setpoint
always counters the weight loss and sooner or later (usually
in less than six months and sometimes in a few weeks) they
are right back up where they were. Their setpoint keeps
them in a certain range, and they can't go below that range
for very long.

Not only that, but if you're not careful, you can *raise
your setpoint still higher* by eating too much rich food that
is high in fat, and particularly sweets. And as if that isn't
bad enough, even artificial sweeteners, which have no calories to speak of, can drive your setpoint up![2]

In an interview with *Executive Fitness Newsletter,* Joel Gurin, coauthor of *The Dieter's Dilemma,* explained that the absence of calories in artificial sweeteners doesn't really help because the taste of the sweetener acts on the brain in such a way that it raises the setpoint and makes the body want to store more fat.[3]

All of this seems to send us back to square one. Those of us with a high setpoint are predestined to have a certain percentage of fat and a certain weight. Is there nothing we can do? Actually there are several ways to turn down your fat thermostat. Brain or intestinal-bypass surgery are options, but not very attractive or advisable. Bennett and Gurin also believe that the use of chemicals, such as those in diet pills, can turn down the setpoint—as long as you keep taking the pills. Nicotine also seems to affect the setpoint and many smokers can testify that when they give up smoking they gain weight.

None of the above are very healthy approaches to the problem, however. That leaves—you guessed it—*exercise.* Bennett and Gurin believe that aerobic exercise acts like a handle to crank down your setpoint.[4] As long as you maintain an adequate exercise program (at least thirty minutes of aerobic activity four or five times a week), you can eat normally and maintain your lower setpoint. Stop the exercise program, however, and your setpoint creeps right back up again to its old level.

One major reason aerobic exercise effectively lowers your setpoint is that it increases your metabolic rate. You have probably heard (or used) the typical argument given by people who are overfat: "It's my metabolism—it's just slow." We also hear over and over that skinny people eat more than Mr. and Mrs. Flab, but the skinny ones never gain an ounce. And for the most part this is true. The startling but proven fact is that fat persons, on an average, eat *less* than slender ones!

It is true that sometimes the slender person can thank his lucky genetic stars that he can eat all he wants but never gain weight. But all slender people aren't necessarily programmed from birth to be that way. Through an active life-style and exercise, they have changed their metabolism to include a predominance of fat-burning enzymes.

Enzymes act as catalysts in your body to stimulate the fat-burning process. Your body is like a factory that burns two kinds of fuel: sugar and fat. Without going into a short course on biochemistry, it is essentially accurate to say that people who are overfat have a predominance of sugar (glucose) burning enzymes; people who are fit and in the ideal range of body fat have a predominance of fat (fatty acid) burning enzymes.

To come back to the comparison of your body to a factory, remember that we eat three basic kinds of food: fat, carbohydrates, and proteins. Your "factory" converts all three of these foods into body-building materials and fuel. The fuel is produced in two forms: fatty acids and glucose. When you eat fat (a lot of butter, for example) little conversion is necessary, and the butter becomes fatty-acid fuel. When you eat protein (for example, eggs) or carbohydrates (for example, bread), your body's conversion machinery breaks these foods down into glucose (a fancy word for sugar).

What happens, then, if your daily routine is not very active? (Remember, by "active" I mean some form of aerobic exercise for at least twelve minutes at a time.) If you are not active, your body burns little or none of the fatty-acid fuel. Instead, it burns primarily the glucose (sugar). If you overeat even a little bit, the chances are good that your body's boilers will not burn all the glucose. At this point another conversion process takes place in your cells. Any excess unburned glucose is *converted to fat* and stored as flab—on your tummy, arms, legs, or other embarrassing locations. And, needless to say, if you have also eaten a certain amount of fat, the fatty-acid fuel never gets burned at all and it, too, gets stored as more flab.

But when you become more active, particularly with some kind of aerobic exercise, you gain two tremendous benefits:

1. You have more muscles, which you build through the exercise, and your muscles consume more fuel (calories). Your muscles are like motors in your body that burn your fuels—the fats and the glucose.

2. By consistently participating in aerobic exercise, the enzymes in your muscles, where your metabolism takes place, literally shift from the type that function primarily to burn glucose (made from carbohydrates or protein) to the kind that burn fat as the main fuel.

This shift from sugar-burning to fat-burning enzymes that occurs through exercise is why a world-class runner like Frank Shorter (winner of the gold medal in the marathon at the Munich Olympics) burns as much as 80 percent fat as fuel while he is just sitting down. Through his extensive running and training programs he has built a slender yet muscular physique that promotes the burning of fat.

Keep remembering that the key to having all of this work for you is to *stay with your aerobic exercise program.* If you go on it for a while, then quit for a while, and then try to go back on it, you will have disappointing results. It seems that the fat-burning enzymes are unstable. Your body soon switches back to the sugar-burning enzymes if you sit around for very long. But even gentle running or brisk walking will at least keep you with 50 percent fat-burning enzymes and only 50 percent sugar-burning enzymes.

Quit your aerobic exercise program, however, and the percentages will go more into the 70 to 90 percent sugar-burning and only 10 to 30 percent fat-burning enzymes. And, of course, as you allow your body "factory" to convert over to burning more sugar than fat, your setpoint acts accordingly and puts more fat back on your body—back to that genetically predetermined range that keeps you anywhere from a little too flabby to a great deal overweight.

Most of what I have said above is a very simplistic explanation of the many complex activities that go on in your body all the time. If you want to know more, I highly recommend Covert Bailey's excellent book *Fit or Fat*. Bailey's nontechnical writing and clear diagramming will give a good picture of how your "factory" operates. But if you have had enough talk about enzymes and fuel conversion just remember one basic fact: *Fit persons are fatty-acid burners and fat persons are sugar burners.* You can change from an overfat person to a fit person by exercising and building the kind of enzymes that burn fat rather than sugar. Over a period of time, aerobic exercises will literally change your metabolism and make you a more efficient fat user. You get a higher metabolic rate with consistent exercise.

As I said earlier in this chapter, the setpoint theory is unproven. Some people call it pure speculation, and others even label it quasiscientific nonsense. Nonetheless, evidence from scientific studies (described in great detail by Bennett and Gurin in *The Dieter's Dilemma*) is piling up. And regardless of what you might think of this setpoint theory, there is overwhelming evidence that continued aerobic exercise reduces fat content in your body and brings your weight down as well. There's also overwhelming evidence that trying to lose fat and weight by diet only is a difficult, if not hopeless, task.

If you aren't so sure you agree with the setpoint theory of Bennett and Gurin, I offer you the "exercise level theory" of Jim Krafft, which simply says:

Fat content (flab) accumulates or disappears in direct proportion to the amount of aerobic activity engaged in.

I have seen it work in my own life; I have seen it work in the lives of hundreds of people here at Oral Roberts University. And it can work for you—if you are willing to do just a little work yourself!

16

Why Being Well Includes More Than Low Fat Percentage

Earlier in this book I stated that any percentage of body fat above 24 percent for men and 34 percent for women is in the category of "sick," or disease producing. The opposite of sickness is wellness, and one of the major goals of this book is to promote wellness to anyone who will listen.

Fortunately wellness is an increasingly important concept in our thinking in America. A priority item for me is serving on the board of directors of the Organization of Wellness Networks, a group of experts and specialists who come from many disciplines that have to do with health and fitness. This group meets annually to exchange information and discuss methods of promoting wellness among the general public.

In the last few years I have observed that when I talk

about wellness, people are much more apt to listen. Medical care is costing more than we as a nation can afford. The alternative to medical care is the prevention of illness, and it's a far more attractive alternative emotionally as well as economically. None of us desires illness, yet our life-styles continually cause us to be ill. We spend billions of dollars annually to fight illness and bring ourselves back to point zero—not being sick. Not being sick is often referred to erroneously as "health," but recovery from disease is far from a total state of health. Our birthright as human beings is creative well-being, or moving into what I call "positive wellness." Helping people achieve creative or positive wellness is my purpose in life.

Wellness includes a lot of things. It encompasses stress management, job satisfaction, the environment, social relationships, and other factors, but none of these is central to who a person really is. I believe man lives in a body, but he is essentially a spirit with intellect, will, and emotions. Wellness of the spirit is the hub about which every other facet of wellness revolves. You can be totally free of excess fat, but if you are in the midst of a spiritual desert you are in a far worse state than many obese people. Personally, I believe the human spirit is only well when it is properly related to God. The vital first step in wellness is faith.

Bruce Larson has written the book *There's a Lot More to Health Than Not Being Sick.* The title of Bruce's book rings true. I strongly recommend that you read it. You should be well in every aspect of your being, not merely your fat percentage.

If wellness becomes a cult of physical health only, it has badly missed its purpose. A human being is a whole person with many facets. The body is important, but it is not primary. If the advice in this book produces an active slender person who is nevertheless miserable, I have failed.

God has created a marvelous physical house in which we can live, and we have the opportunity to assist Him in its care. I believe we honor God when we do all we can to keep that house—the body—well and healthy.

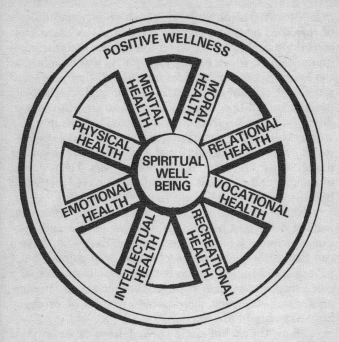

Wellness of the spirit is the hub about which other facets of wellness revolve.

It is not too surprising that depression is one of the major illnesses in America. More than 50 percent of our population experiences significant depression at some time during life. Many of these depressed people are fat. Since the most widely documented help for depression is walking, slow jogging, or other aerobic activity, we are able to treat effectively two conditions at once: being overfat and being depressed.

I have personal knowledge of both conditions. When I was in my late forties, my first wife died of cancer, and I went through a period of typical depression. Also, I had periodic bouts with tension and anxiety that built up through job pressures.

My own passion for jogging comes from a multiplicity of reasons. I began around age fifty, largely because I felt something could be done about some minor electrocardiogram changes, which I discovered when I was examined at the Kenneth Cooper Aerobics Institute. At that time I had a body fat content of almost 24 percent and weighed 206 pounds. In addition I was suffering from an arthritic condition that developed after I was exposed to dysentery on a trip to Mexico. My rheumatologist told me that I couldn't do any walking or jogging for at least six months, but after a brief stay in the hospital, I started anyway. The first year of walking and jogging was difficult, but I stayed motivated because I wanted to become more fit and healthy.

Now I run slow and long, purely for fun. I find that jogging is the best method for releasing tension and emotional pressure. Even now, on some rare days, I will have a run that is totally uncomfortable and even painful, but I have learned the difference between harming myself and going through a certain amount of beneficial pain. In some mysterious way even those occasional runs of drudgery have a quality of joy.

Many times, but not always, I have experienced a mystical, almost unbelievable, breakthrough experience. This usually occurs about forty minutes into a jog. Now I much prefer jogging or running to competitive sports like racquetball or tennis. In fact, I now regularly give up opportunities for racquetball or tennis because I find these somewhat boring as compared to a slow, relaxing run.

I am not enthusiastic about competition, but I still enter long distance races purely for the comradery and excitement of being with others. Even though I finished last in my first marathon (26.2 miles), I enjoyed a tremendous sense of accomplishment, completeness, and exhilaration. I have now completed six marathons.

I still battle anxiety and tension, which are the precursors of depression. That's why I usually do my jogging after work, when I am able to regain my equilibrium and feelings of well-being. I find it difficult to explain clearly my passion for jogging. Perhaps the most important point for me is that in my daily exercise experiences I find myself genuinely close to God.

My aerobic activities have provided many direct physical benefits. My arthritis is gone and my electrocardiogram reads perfectly. But even without the specific physical results, I believe I would continue jogging just for the relaxation, clearing of the mind, and the outstanding spiritual rewards.

I have written this book with the sole purpose of trying to convince you to start aerobics or to keep going in what you may have started already. I firmly believe the key to wellness is aerobic exercise.

17

A Final Word on the First Word

The message of this book was epitomized recently when one of my colleagues, Dr. Lynn M. Nichols, was checking over my manuscript. He was reviewing chapter one, "The First Word Is Not *Diet*," and remarked, "Isn't this a mistake? You are saying that the essence of losing fat is exercise. I thought the essence of losing weight was a sensible diet."

To correct that kind of misconception is precisely why I wrote this book. It has been so engrained in us that diet is the way to lose fat that it is extremely hard to get across that the real way to lose fat is by regular endurance exercise.

I will say it one more time. *Dieting is helpful, but the way to lose weight, the way to lose fat and keep it off, is through exercise.* And by exercise I mean aerobic activity, carried out regularly for the rest of your life. Aerobic exercise is slow, easy, and continuous and it builds the fat-

2. See, for example, Covert Bailey, *Fit or Fat?* (Boston: Houghton Mifflin Co., 1978), chapters 23 and 24.

   Another excellent little book is *Eating Smart* by Judith Stern, Sc.D., nutrition consultant to Campbell Soup Company's Turnaround Program, and R. V. Denenberg. To order, write to: Box 8688, Clinton, Iowa 52736 ($1.00 each).

Chapter 13

1. Charles T. Kuntzleman, Ed.D., *Your Active Way to Weight Control* (Spring Arbor, Mich.: Fitness Finders, 1980). To order, write to: Fitness Finders, 133 Teft Road, P.O. Box 507, Spring Arbor, Michigan 49283 ($1.00 each).

Chapter 14

1. Mervyn G. Hardinge, M.D., ed., "Obesity: You Can Lose Weight," *Life and Health,* vol. II, 1st. edition (1974), p. 10.
2. Hardinge, "Obesity: You Can Lose Weight," p. 16.

Chapter 15

1. William Bennett, M.D., and Joel Gurin, *The Dieter's Dilemma: Eating Less and Weighing More* (New York: Basic Books, Inc., 1982). In chapter one, "Fat and Fate," Bennett and Gurin present the thesis that reducing diets are not effective for weight control because of the body's predetermined setpoint, which dictates how much fat one should carry.
2. Bennett and Gurin, *The Dieter's Dilemma,* p. 100.
3. "On Losing Weight: Is Fat Fate?", *Executive Fitness Newsletter,* vol. 13, no. 20 (October 2, 1982), Rodale Press, Inc.
4. Bennett and Gurin, *The Dieter's Dilemma,* p. 7.

For Further Reading

Bailey, Covert. *Fit or Fat?* Boston: Houghton Mifflin Co., 1978.

Bennett, William and Gurin, Joel. *The Dieter's Dilemma: Eating Less and Weighing More.* New York: Basic Books, Inc., 1982.

Cooper, Kenneth. *The Aerobics Way.* New York: M. Evans, and Co., 1977.

Eargle, Jon. *Healing Where You Hurt—on the Inside.* Broken Arrow, Okla.: PTL Productions, 1981.

Higdon, Hal. *Fitness After Forty.* Mountain View, Calif.: Anderson World, Inc., 1977.

Hill, Harold. *How to Flip Your Flab—Forever.* Plainfield, N.J.: Logos International, 1979.

Kostrubala, Thaddeus. *The Joy of Running.* New York: J. B. Lippincott Co., 1976; Pocket Books, Inc., 1977.

Kuntzleman, Charles T., and the Editors of Consumer Guide. *The Complete Book of Walking.* New York: Pocket Books, Inc., 1982.

Kuntzleman, Charles T., Ed.D. *Your Active Way to Weight Control.* Spring Arbor, Mich.: Fitness Finders, 1980.

Larson, Bruce. *There's a Lot More to Health Than Not Being Sick.* Waco, Tex.: Word Books, 1981.

Losing weight is accomplished through regular, sustained, enjoyable exercise.

losing, or fat-burning, enzymes. As Covert Bailey has said, "You become a better butter burner." Exercise increases your metabolism.

The whole message of this book is that losing weight and fat is not done through restrictive dieting. It is done by having fun through regular, sustained, enjoyable exercise. So burn that butter, Baby! And while you burn it, have fun and get slim.

God bless you as you become a winner at the losing game!

Source Notes

Chapter 3

1. Dr. Bailey's fine book makes an excellent companion to the present volume. See Covert Bailey, *Fit or Fat?* (Boston: Houghton Mifflin Co., 1978).

Chapter 4

1. Barbara C. O'Conner, "Body Fat and Its Effects on the Health of a Group of College Coeds As Shown by an Investigation of Their Visits to the Health Clinic," a thesis prepared in partial completion of a master's degree in public health, 1980.

Chapter 5

1. Donald Cooley, *How to Lose Weight* (New York: Random House, 1956), p. 13.
2. Cooley, *How to Lose Weight*, page 12.
3. Hal Higdon, "Slow Down," *Parade* (August 30, 1981).

Chapter 9

1. Hal Higdon, "Ten Most Asked Questions About Exercise," *The Physician and Sportsmedicine* (September 1980), p. 112.

Chapter 10

1. Robert Atkins, *Dr. Atkins' Diet Revolution* (New York: Bantam Books, Inc., 1981).